Jersey

Stories of Authentic New Jersey People & Events

By: Maureen K. Wlodarczyk

Jersey! Then . . . Again

All Rights Reserved

Copyright © 2014

This book may not be reproduced, transmitted, or stored in whole or in part, by any means including graphic, electronic or mechanical without the express written consent of the author or publisher except in the case of brief quotations embodied in critical articles and reviews.

Also by Maureen Wlodarczyk:

Past-Forward:

A Three-Decade & Three-Thousand-Mile Journey Home

Young & Wicked:

The Death of a Wayward Girl

Canary in a Cage:

The Smith-Bennett Murder Case

With gratitude for the opportunity to wander through the past and share the stories of decades and centuries gone by . . .

Contents

Peter Graham – Phrenologist	1
Decoration Day to Memorial Day	6
Peter Henderson – Horticulturist	10
The Vagabond Hurricane of 1903	15
1922 Auto Show	19
NJ Actresses Selene Johnson & Carrie Ewald	24
Andrew Corcoran – NJ Entrepreneur & Activist	30
Armistice Day to Veterans Day	35
1906 Disasters & NJ Charity	39
NJ Artists Arnold Wydeveld & August Will	43
Charles Schreyvogel – Hoboken Painter	48
Dr. Oliver P. Brown – Herbal Medicine Practitioner	53
Fred Astaire & Young Gus Suckow	58
Halloween in Days Gone By	63
Hoboken: Home of Competitive Baseball	68
Hot Air Ballooning in New Jersey	73
Spanish Influenza Epidemic	77
Julius Fehr – Hoboken Doctor & Inventor	81

Karl Bitter – Weehawken Sculptor	87
Lady Liberty	93
Loewus Brothers – Liquor Distributors	98
Mother's Day	102
New Jersey Wheelmen	106
Oscar Schmidt – Musical Instrument Maker	111
NJ Photographers Stieglitz & Gubelman	116
Simon "King" Kelly – Weehawken Political Force	122
Hudson County Theatres & Movie Houses	126
The Titanic Disaster	131
Rosie the Riveter – NJ Women in the War Effort	135
The Featherstone Gang	139
19th Century NJ Yacht Clubs	143
NJ Irish-American Boxers McCarthy & Burns	148
Isaac Edge – 1812 Drummer Boy & Pyrotechnist	153
Snake Hill – An All-Too-Common NJ Legacy	159
Weehawken's Eldorado Park	165
Votes for Women – NJ Suffragettes	170

Introduction

I am a Jersey "girl" born of entwined multi-ethnic family lines, for which I am ever-grateful. Thanksgiving meant inhaling the aroma of chicken cacciatore in one grandmother's kitchen and digging into a heap of stuffing, roast turkey and cranberry sauce at the table of the other. Then there was the sauerbraten . . . .

It is evident from my writing that I am addicted to history and the stories of our collective past. Those true stories of long-gone people, places and events can still entertain, inform, provoke thought and pique curiosity. I tend not to write about the famous (or infamous) stories that have survived the passage of time, but rather about people and things that have been lost to time. I am drawn to those dusty jewels I often discover in old books and newspapers that serve to transport us back and allow us to experience a real view of life as it was. That color and context make all the difference.

This collection of New Jersey stories, originally written for newspapers and my blog, features the good, the bad, the bizarre, the amusing, and often surprising people and events of our Garden State. I hope you enjoy these true tales. You can read more of my stories about New Jersey history and my genealogy adventures in *Garden State Legacy* magazine (www.gardenstatelegacy.com), a great publication devoted to sharing stories of New Jersey's past.

Maureen

Peter Graham: Phrenologist

While researching my book, *Canary in a Cage: The Smith-Bennett Murder Case*, based on the true story of a young woman accused of killing her Jersey City police officer husband in 1878, I read dozens and dozens of newspaper articles about the murder and multiple trials that followed. That 19th century press coverage made for fascinating reading and introduced me to a cast of characters whose real lives rivaled anything a fiction writer might dream up. Among them was one "Professor" Graham, a Hudson County phrenologist, temperance activist, and something of a Victorian-era life coach.

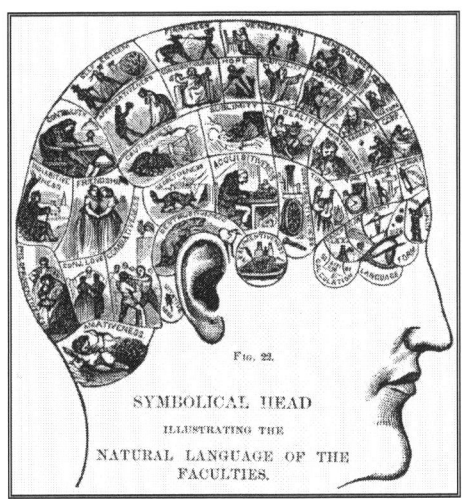

Phrenology, quite the thing in the late 1800s, has been described as a pseudoscience of the 18th and 19th centuries based on the belief that a determination of a person's mental capacity and character (or predisposition to criminality) could be made by examining the skull and interpreting its bumps and depressions. Talk about "getting your head examined!"

Peter Graham was born in Scotland in 1833 and married his wife Ellen in Edinburgh in 1851. In 1869, the Grahams and their 8 children, including 4-year-old Abraham Lincoln Graham, booked passage in steerage on the S. S. Helvetia out of Liverpool, England, and landed in New York City on October 1st. When the census-taker made his rounds ten months later, the Graham family was living in Jersey City and Peter gave his occupation as "temperance lecturer." Quite a transformation from the occupation of "laborer" he gave when booking passage on the Helvetia a year earlier.

S.S. HELVETIA

In August 1870, Graham gave a spirited temperance speech attended by hundreds in Bayonne at the request of the Sons of Temperance organization and followed that with another at Currie's Woods a week later. He was also engaged by the Gospel Temperance Union to lecture on the ills of alcohol at the local Republican Club's Wigwam headquarters. It was reported that he gave a rousing cautionary talk about a devastated woman whose husband and son were in the grip of addiction to rum.

Graham soon widened the array of topics for his lectures and often included phrenology concepts and examinations as well. He also offered phrenological classes in a variety of places in New Jersey and as far away as New England and Michigan. In 1876, his Paterson students arranged a phrenological tea party attended by over 100 people to honor Graham. Two years later, students in his Boston class, where the "Professor" had done over 80 lectures, presented him with a set of silver phrenological tools (calipers, ruler and tape measure) in a Moroccan leather case in appreciation of his work.

Graham reportedly once examined the skull of a woman who attended one of his talks with her husband and pronounced that she must have a "most violent temper." The woman turned to her husband asking him to confirm that Graham's assessment was wrong. The husband made no response but attendees said he told them she was subject to tantrums and throwing things.

Graham frequently gave talks on marriage, contrasting potential husbands with flat heads versus those having "honest" heads with appropriate width and height. The flat-headed male, according to the Professor, has character flaws that show themselves in childhood and result in a suitor who has several ladies on a string at one time and, due to lack of moral "faculties," is prone to excessive drinking and spousal abuse. He encouraged ladies to feel the heads of their beaus before accepting a marriage proposal and demonstrated how to do so using life-size models of skulls, concluding by saying that a woman would be better off marrying a gorilla than a flat-headed man.

One of Graham's lectures in 1878 included a phrenological discussion of the young accused murderess, Jenny Smith, whose story I wrote about in *Canary in a Cage*. Just days after her arrest, Graham gave a talk in Jersey City titled "People Who Murder." He discussed how the heads of some celebrated murderers conformed to each other and, turning his attention to the case of Jenny Smith, concluded that although she might be a "loose" woman, if her ears were placed high up on her head, she was not a murderer.

Peter Graham died in Jersey City in 1880, only ten years after immigrating to America. His obituary in a local newspaper described him as "a man of marked ability," an "ardent advocate of temperance," but "eccentric in his manners."

Decoration Day to Memorial Day

The sesquicentennial of the American Civil War has fueled renewed interest in the epic conflict that threatened to irreparably tear apart the fabric of our nation. Historians, authors, military and veterans groups, academic institutions and museums are offering programs, exhibits, re-enactments and books about that war, ensuring that this important story is retold and remembered. This is especially timely on the last Monday in May when we celebrate Memorial Day, the day we honor members of our military who died while serving our country.

Memorial Day, originally called Decoration Day, was born in the immediate aftermath of the Civil War when the families of war dead began the practice of bringing flowers to decorate the graves of loved ones lost in that conflict. In May 1868, the commander-in-chief of the Grand Army of the Republic (GAR), the veterans' organization for those who served in the Union Army, issued a proclamation requesting that "Decoration Day" be observed throughout the United States. Commemoration activities in the North in those early years often included rhetoric aimed at Southerners whose secession and rebellion was seen as treasonous. Reconciliation came slowly and painfully on both sides as the years passed.

In May 1868, Decoration Day services and the placing of flowers on veterans' graves took place in Hudson County under the auspices of the local GAR chapter. Among the dignitaries and organizations participating that year were the Bergen, Hudson City and General Philip Kearny GAR posts, rifle corps, the Father Matthew Society, Concordia Glee Club, the mayors and council members of Hudson, Hoboken, Bergen and Jersey City and the Police Board. A long line of horse carriages formed at 1pm for the procession leaving from Montgomery Street in Jersey City and heading to the various local cemeteries. The commemoration activities the following year expanded to include horse-drawn hearses carrying the flowers, and Civil War soldiers and sailors, members of the local clergy, distinguished orators, Reinhart's Band, the Hudson County Artillery, the 4th Regiment of the N.J. National Guard and citizens in their own carriages. Around the County, flags were lowered to half-mast throughout the day and businesses and public offices were closed.

In May 1870, Decoration Day observances took on a special, solemn significance as the body of a Jersey City man and Union soldier, Stewart Turner, was returned home for burial at the New York Bay Cemetery. Turner, a Private in Company K of the N.J. 2nd Infantry Regiment, had died in July 1865 at a hospital in Alexandria, Virginia and had initially been interred there. His body was exhumed nearly five years later and returned home for reburial in Jersey City. Reports at the time described huge crowds that came out to see the procession that included a large horse-drawn stage carrying a group of young ladies charged with placing flowers on the graves of the dead Union soldiers at the New York Bay, Jersey City Harsimus and local Catholic cemeteries. The hearse carrying Private Turner's remains was provided by Wandle & Son Undertakers of Montgomery Street and was drawn by "four splendid grays." A banner in front of Hose Company No.3 displayed the following words: "Let angels spread their wings above, let flowers forever bloom; Let bays, green bays, spring up to mark the martyrs sacred tomb."

Awaiting the burial procession at New York Bay Cemetery were hundreds of local citizens who had traveled by carriage, trolley or on foot. Near the cemetery, local officials, speakers, and clergy congregated on a platform in front of which military representatives and bands were stationed and ceremonies took place. The observances concluded with the singing of "My Country 'Tis of Thee."

In searching for my own family history I discovered, just a few years ago, that my Irish-born great-great-grandfather, John J. Flannelly, who came to Jersey City in the late 1840s fleeing the Irish potato famine, fought in the Civil War as a Private in the N.J. 6th Infantry Regiment. Like Stewart Turner, my great-great-grandfather was hospitalized while his unit was engaged in Virginia. Fortunately for me, John survived to return home to Downtown Jersey City, marry and raise a large family.

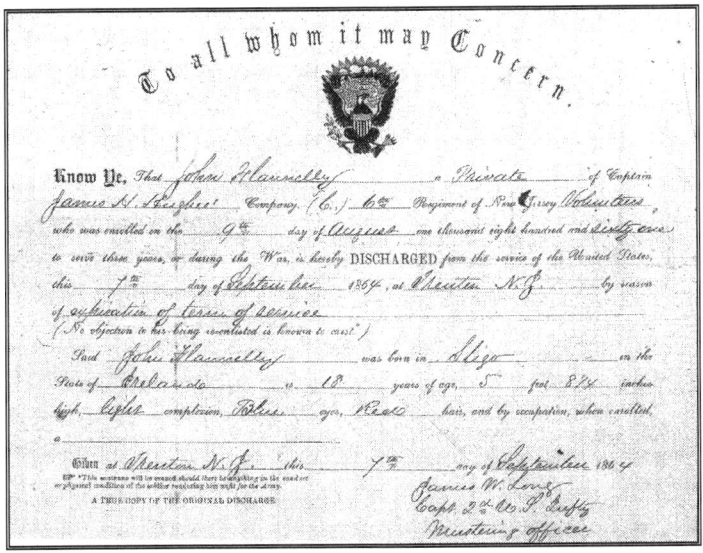

Today, nearly a century-and-a-half after Private Stewart Turner's remains were laid to rest in Jersey City, American cemeteries continue to receive members of our brave military that died in wars, conflicts and acts of terrorism around the world. As we look forward to the holiday weekend and the start of the summer season, let us pause to honor the memory and sacrifices of our men and women in uniform.

Peter Henderson: Horticulturist

In 2011 and 2012, I participated in the annual *Tale of Our City* book festival in Jersey City held in Van Vorst Park, the lovely, historic Victorian gem that has been adorning Downtown for 160 years. The development of the park resulted from the open space preservation interest of Cornelius Van Vorst who donated the land, and the horticultural expertise of Peter Henderson who created and executed the landscape design. So, who was Peter Henderson: immigrant, market gardener, florist, and the force behind what would become a national seed and plant business supplied by acres of glass hothouses he built in Jersey City Heights?

According to 19th century publications, Henderson was born near Edinburgh, Scotland in 1823. His father was a land-steward for a local "gentleman." At 16, Henderson became an apprentice gardener and within two years won two medals from the Botanical Society of Edinburgh in recognition of his work. At the age of 20, he left Scotland for New York with not much more than a small amount of pocket money and those two medals he had won. He obtained employment in New York, working for gardeners and florists, saving as much as he could until he was able to go into business for himself. He relocated to Jersey City in 1847, buying land on Wayne, Monmouth and Mercer Streets and launched his market gardening enterprise. That was followed by his opening a floral shop and selling seeds. From that, some years later, was born his seed and plant business, Peter Henderson & Co., located on Cortlandt Street in Manhattan and offering its products via color lithograph catalogs.

By the 1880s, Henderson's greenhouses in the Heights were said to be the largest in the world, covering over 5 acres, managed by a staff of some 100 men, and described as measuring 100 feet long by 20 feet wide. To achieve needed shading, Henderson explained that the glass was treated with a solution of naptha mixed with a small amount of lead with the consistency of "thin milk," a method low in cost and lasting an entire season until the frost in the fall. On the same property, there was a 300 foot "propagating house," a "cold grapery" with arched roof, and large outdoor flower beds described as a most beautiful sight when in bloom. The greenhouses and surrounding grounds became such a popular draw that, in 1879, a notice appeared in a local newspaper stating that "the great number of people" visiting the hothouses on Sundays "has become such an annoyance that the custom has been stopped" and signs were subsequently posted indicating no admission on that day.

Henderson was also a frequent speaker at horticultural gatherings and the author of several books on gardening including *Practical Floriculture, Gardening for Pleasure,* and the *Handbook of Plants* and wrote hundreds of articles on gardening topics that appeared in newspapers and periodicals, among those an article that told of his experiments with carnivorous plants.

Beyond his success and renown, Peter Henderson was also a generous local citizen and employer. He was often mentioned in Hudson County newspapers of the day for his donations of flowers for local events and to the City Hospital. He was also a founder of the Bergen Savings Bank and when that failed, he and his partners reportedly reimbursed their depositors from their own funds.

In 1874, an article titled "An Ungrateful Young Rascal" appeared in the local press. An 18-year-old boy named Reeves had worked for Henderson at his New York store. Suspected of theft there, Henderson transferred him to work in the Jersey City gardens rather than dismissing him. As soon as Reeves began working in Jersey City, a large number of flowers started going missing daily. Surveillance caught Reeves in the act of stealing the plants (which he then sold in New York). Instead of having him arrested, Henderson gave him $2.00 and a talking to. The following night Reeves was caught stealing 400 roses and was arrested.

Henderson, who was fond of saying he had never been sick a day in his life, fell ill with pneumonia and died at his home on Arlington Avenue in January 1890 at the age of 66. At his funeral, the presiding minister praised Henderson saying: "It was his pluck, industry and capacity for work that made him successful. He did not turn things into gold by merely touching them. He had the true scientific spirit and a profound love of nature . . ."

The Vagabond Hurricane of 1903

October 2012 brought Superstorm Sandy to New Jersey, an event that shattered lives and houses and left an indelible mark on our state. A dear friend and my god-daughter each lost their home to a river surge in Middlesex County. I count myself among the fortunate who endured nothing worse than a week or so of cold, dark nights and cold morning showers in the aftermath of Sandy. My husband is a managing engineer and storm response team leader for my local electric company. He and his colleagues worked 16-hour days assessing damage and coordinating restoration efforts. The road back, literally and figuratively, winds on for many people who are still displaced and struggling to make their way forward. For the next few minutes, let me take you back more than a century ago to another time when a wayward, willful storm traveled a similar path and made landfall in New Jersey.

In September 1903, the so-called "Vagabond" hurricane meandered on a west/northwest track originating in the area of Antigua, passing south of Bermuda and then curving northward and heading for Atlantic City. It made landfall there with estimated winds of 80 mph. Fishing piers and ocean pavilions in Atlantic City were damaged or destroyed, wires went down all along the New Jersey coastline, and damage reports were provided via observations made using trains.

In Hudson County, local newspapers reported the severe, widespread property damage resulting from the hurricane's high-velocity winds and driving rain. According to those reports, "school children were blown about the streets, women were thrown off their feet, trolley car traffic was suspended, buildings were unroofed, and streets were turned into raging torrents." Trees and wires were "blown down" and boats along the New York Bay shore-front were pushed up on land and "reduced to kindling wood."

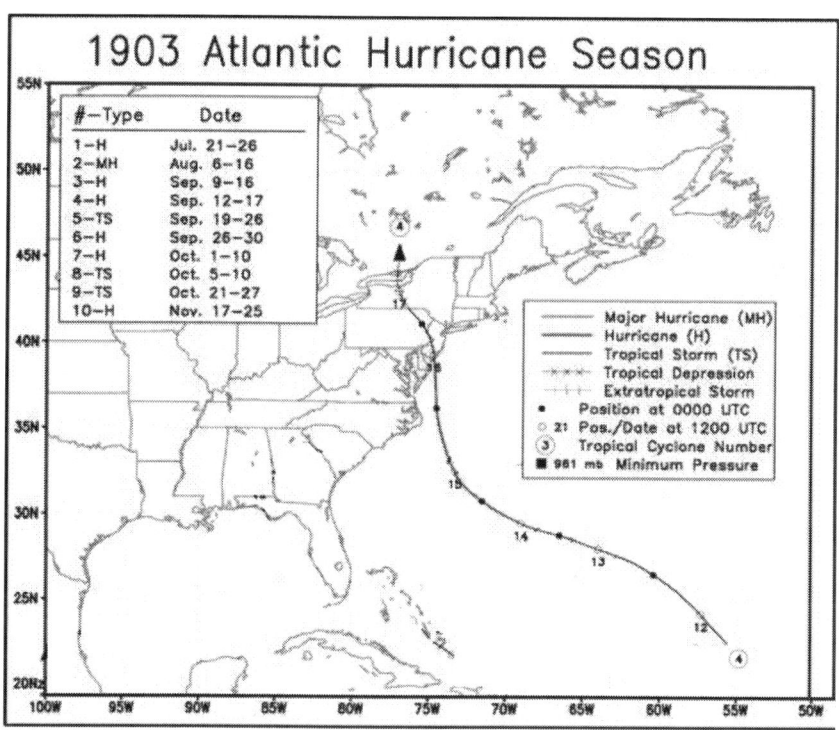

At the City Hospital in Jersey City, havoc ensued as the dispensary was flooded, the sewer backed up and patients were drenched as the wind-driven rain got into the "ramshackle" buildings from "a thousand openings" around windows and in the roof. Unable to abate the flooding in any other way, hospital management instructed staff to bore holes in the wooden floor to allow the water to escape. The Hudson County Court House suffered considerable damage with flooded courtrooms, broken skylights, and large trees downed as did City Halls in both Bayonne and Jersey City. The Oakley Baseball Club's grandstand on Ninth Street near Brunswick Street in Jersey City, newly-built to seat 1,000 spectators, was demolished to a "pile of lumber."

A two-story frame house at 59 Terrace Avenue in Jersey City was lifted from its foundation and "sailed through the air for a distance of ten feet" before landing in a neighbor's yard. Mrs. John Ryan, Mrs. Frank Kennedy, and 8 children were in the house at the time and other than being somewhat in shock, survived the incident unscathed. On Ravine Road, storm sewers were overwhelmed and the accumulating waters thrust manhole covers aside as geysers sprouted in their place.

Among the parallels between the Vagabond and Sandy were the loss of electricity and massive disruption to public transportation. In 1903, the Hudson County press reported on "snapped electric wires" and lineman out on the streets reconnecting wires immediately after the gale-force winds subsided. The power company plant at Wayne and Fremont Streets in Jersey City had been knocked out by flooding but was restored to operation quickly due to "energetic" efforts by the plant superintendent. Trolley service, an essential mode of public transportation, was crippled as wires came down. Rushing water derailed cars and left passengers standing on their seats as the trolleys were stranded on flooded streets.

Then, as now, as soon as the immediate danger from the storm had passed, restoration and recovery efforts were quickly underway. Amid all the bad news being reported, one Hudson County newspaper, quoting the maxim "it is an ill wind that blows no good," observed that painters, glaziers, wallpaper hangers and plasterers would "reap profits" as a result of the storm. Talk about cock-eyed optimism!

1922 Auto Show

In these days of economic anemia, posturing politicians and a plethora of pundits paid to enlighten us on the cable and traditional networks, comparisons of today's troubles with the dark years of the Depression have been a frequent theme. In both cases, it seems that a decade of excess gave birth to a financial bubble that painfully burst much like when, as children, we (over)blew a big, pink gum bubble that exploded, leaving a stringy mess on face and hair.

The decade preceding the onset of the Depression, the Roaring Twenties, was fueled by the post-World War I boom, the dawn of the age of everything "modern," and the risky and risqué subculture resulting from Prohibition. It was also the era when American women won the right to vote. Speaking of 1920s "modernity," women, and voting, let me tell you about the thoroughly modern 1922 Hudson County Automobile Association Show, where a fashion "pageant" complete with supermodels was part of the week-long event held at the Fourth Regiment Armory in Jersey City.

The Armory was decorated in an oriental garden motif with a large electric fountain, Japanese wisteria and lanterns accenting the floor-plan where local car dealers displayed 100 vehicles representing 32 makes of the latest passenger automobiles including Studebaker, Hudson, Hupmobile, Buick, Cadillac, Packard, Auburn, Oldsmobile,

Nash, Essex, Dodge, Lincoln and Rickenbacker. The balcony of the Armory showcased displays of auto accessories and the ceiling was covered in a blue canopy creating the effect of an open sky. Local newspapers described the auto show as "the most gorgeous ever," drawing dealers and attendees from the greater metropolitan area and growing "to the point of national importance."

In addition to the crowds of gentlemen who turned out for the show, attendance swelled as the ladies of Hudson County came out in large numbers for the daily fashion pageants that had been incorporated into the show. To rounds of loud applause, twelve well-known professional models promenaded at 3pm each day wearing the latest in daywear, evening gowns, "sports frocks," hats, shoes and hosiery. A local paper commented that one of the models, dressed in a "negligee effect shift" was quite a hit. The fashion shows were presented in conjunction with Max Herzberg, art director of the *Pictorial Review*, the most popular women's magazine of the day. One of the notable models was Mimi Palmieri, who also supervised the daily fashion shows. Like many supermodels of today, Mimi parlayed her modeling fame into acting and appeared in several films including playing opposite Alfred Lunt in *The Ragged Edge* (1923) and *Second Youth* (1924).

Mimi Palmieri

Daily events at the auto show also included special evenings for local groups such as the Lions Club, Elks, Chamber of Commerce, Rotary/Kiwanis and Automobile Club when members attended as guests of the Automobile Association. This was one of the ways the auto show had the effect of community building, not just business building. While the show promoted closer relationships between car manufacturers and local car dealers as well as car dealers and car buyers, it also drew the local community as a social and entertainment event. Activities specifically targeted at the ladies were the icing on the cake.

One of those activities was a vote to select the "Most Popular Woman Driver in Hudson County." Show attendees received a voting coupon with their box office ticket on which they wrote the name of the lady of their choice. As the competition heated up, daily vote counts were tallied and reported by the local press. The lead seesawed back and forth between two ladies, one from Jersey City and the other from Bayonne.

The final vote count found Bayonne's Henrietta Stabile the victor with 811 votes. Miss Stabile received a fur coat as first prize winner. Jersey City's Mrs. Louis Cosgrove, who lost by only 7 votes, received a fur automobile wrap, both prizes aimed at keeping the lady drivers warm on cold winter days. But there's more.

Henrietta Stabile, a senior at Bayonne High School, made the local paper twice on November 20, 1922. The first article reported that she continued to have the lead in the vote to select the County's most popular woman driver. The second, titled "Crowded Jitney and Auto Bump," reported the collision of a car driven by Miss Stabile and a jitney in Bayonne resulting in slight damage to the vehicles and the jitney passengers being "shaken up" but uninjured. Well, she was voted *most popular* driver . . . not *best* driver.

New Jersey Actresses:

Selene Johnson & Carrie Ewald

Being an unrepentant history addict, I enjoy discovering and reading about people who lived decades ago as I find their lives and times more intriguing and resonant than the exploits of the likes of the Kardashians or Lindsay Lohan. In that spirit, let me tell you the story of two New Jersey actresses who began their stage careers in the 1890s: Selene Johnson and Carrie Ewald. Each was the daughter of a successful local family and each would make a notable marriage, one of those tinged with suspicions about the groom's character.

Selene Johnson was born in 1870 in Bucks County, Pennsylvania. (Most accounts give her birth year as 1876 but, using my genealogy research skills, I found her as a 6-month-old in the 1870 US census.) By 1880, the Johnson family was living on Sixth Street in Jersey City and Selene's father Charles gave his occupation as a railroad "float master" (a person that supervises the movement of freight by barge between a ship and railroad). The Johnson household of six included Selene's two older siblings and an 18-year-old servant named Annie Hankinson.

After graduating from No.2 school and beginning high school in Jersey City, Selene left public school to study music and pursue her theatrical interests. In 1893, she became a student at the Berkeley Lyceum School of Acting in New York, graduated in 1894 and soon joined the Frohman theatrical company performing in Hawaii, New Orleans, Seattle, Portland, British Columbia and even the Sandwich Islands.

Selene Johnson

Her stage career blossomed over the ensuing years and, as the 19th century ended, she became *the* leading lady performing the role of Mercedes opposite the renowned Irish-born actor James O'Neill in his signature role as the Count of Monte Cristo. O'Neill, the father of

Nobel and Pulitzer prize-winning playwright Eugene O'Neill, was synonymous with the legendary hero created by French writer Alexander Dumas, performing the role of the Count more than 5,000 times over two decades to the delight of audiences. O'Neill paid Selene the great compliment of saying she was one of the two most gifted leading ladies he had worked with in his "Count of Monte Cristo" productions. She also appeared with James O'Neill in 1904 in a stage production of Arthur Conan Doyle's "The Adventures of Gerard."

In 1912, Selene married Irish actor F. Lumsden Hare who would be her leading man on and off the stage for many years. Hare, born in Ballingarry, County Tipperary, was the nephew of the Lord

Chancellor of Ireland and a stage actor appearing in London and America. Selene and Lumsden appeared together in various productions and he became a well-known director and actor, appearing in over 140 films. The Hares lived a long life, residing first in New York and then in Los Angeles where each died in the 1960s.

Carrie Ewald was born in Jersey City in 1874 and lived with her family on York Street. Her father, William Ewald, was the prosperous co-owner of Ewald Brothers, a stationery store located on Newark Avenue. Carrie studied elocution at the Hasbrouck Institute in Jersey City and, like her parents, was an accomplished musician. She pursued theatrical training at the Empire Theatre Dramatic School in New York under the direction of noted English actor Nelson Wheatcroft. Like Selene Johnson, after her studies, she joined a Frohman acting company and toured nationally as part of their "Masqueraders" production.

In January 1897, newspapers reported that Carrie Ewald was to marry Count Julian Rado of Budapest, Hungary. The couple was said to have met at a masquerade ball in New York some months earlier when the Count had been captivated by Miss Ewald who was costumed as a water nymph. Along with the news of the engagement the press identified Rado as a man who had been the subject of notoriety in his homeland and had fled to New York where he had been accused of being a swindler and fortune hunter courting the daughter of a wealthy local man.

The following day, Ewald denied the two were engaged or had met at a ball as reported but confirmed that a Mr. Rado was calling on her. For his part, Rado insisted that he was an aspiring law student, never presented himself as nobility and threatened to "prosecute" the source of the story.

Carrie Ewald

> **Actress to Marry a Count.**
> Special to The Inquirer.
> JERSEY CITY, Jan. 1.—It is reported that Miss Carrie Ewald, who until recently was a member of Frohman's "Masqueraders" company, is to be married on February 6 to Count Julian Charles Rado, of Budapesth, Hungary.

Six months after that sensation, Carrie Ewald and Julian Rado did marry in New York City, newspapers reporting that her parents were "satisfied with their daughter's choice of a husband." Carrie apparently left her theatrical life behind when she married. That marriage ended in June 1909 when she passed away at the age of thirty-four. Her obituary described her as the "beloved wife of Julian C. W. Rado." She was laid to rest at New York Bay Cemetery.

Selene Johnson and Carrie Ewald, supported by the resources and encouragement of their families, pursued their dreams of a stage career, first performing for enthusiastic New Jersey locals and then entertaining thousands on stages across the country. Judging by the many laudatory reviews of their performances that appeared in newspapers from coast-to-coast, each did herself proud.

Andrew Corcoran:

New Jersey Entrepreneur & Activist

I heard a cable television pundit remark that we had not really averted going over the "fiscal cliff" but rather swerved at the last minute temporarily avoiding the plunge only to now be hurtling head-on into the debt ceiling crisis. There is no shortage of ideas about how to reduce spending, even if there is no agreement on those recommendations. One of the debt reduction measures being put on the table is the end of subsidies and government funding of private sector solar and wind energy projects.

Windmills have a long history dating back centuries and punctuated by periodic peaks and declines in popularity over the many years since. One of those peak periods occurred in the late 19th and early 20th centuries when the Horseshoe section of Jersey City was home to the Corcoran Windmill Company, named for its entrepreneurial founder, Andrew J. Corcoran. Mr. Corcoran was born in Dublin, Ireland in about 1842 and emigrated to the U.S. with his parents as a teenager in the mid-1850s, living in Brooklyn and in the Albany area where he apprenticed in a blacksmith shop before pursuing work in a machinery manufacturing company. That job led to his working on perfecting a windmill pump for a man named Mills. Mills eventually purchased the manufacturing plant, converting it to produce windmill parts and making Corcoran the plant superintendent. It was there that Corcoran would produce the first self-regulating windmill, an invention that won a prize at a N.Y. State Fair in 1862.

Corcoran Windmill – Long Island NY

Not long after, Corcoran was temporarily blinded by an explosion at the plant and, although he slowly regained some sight, his eyes were permanently damaged. After some years of collaboration with Mills as part of the Empire Windmill Company, Corcoran went into business for himself and, in the late 1880s, opened a factory at Jersey Avenue and Thirteenth Street in Jersey City where both iron and wood-working were done. He was issued multiple patents for his windmill inventions and developments into the early 1890s and he and his family became residents of Jersey City.

ANDREW J. CORCORAN.

Windmills, pumps and water tanks manufactured by the Corcoran Windmill Company were sold to clients around the world and were erected in Italy, India, South America, New Zealand, Egypt, Japan, South Africa and China, where they generated power for irrigation, mining, milling, and other industrial purposes. Right here in New Jersey, Corcoran windmills were in service in Sea Bright and Red Bank among other places. As an employer, Corcoran had a reputation for treating his employees fairly and humanely including paying sick employees and hosting an employee holiday party for 27 consecutive years.

Throughout the first twenty years of the 1900s, Andrew Corcoran was active in Jersey City community affairs, particularly efforts to improve the quality of life in the Horseshoe neighborhood that was home to many other Irish-Americans, including my own great-grandparents. He crusaded for the elevation of the Erie Railroad tracks for citizen safety as well as for the improvement of sewers and sanitation. He also served as president of the Board of Trade.

Corcoran's wife, Eliza Wilder Corcoran, a descendant of an old New York family, became a local philanthropist in Jersey City known for her charitable works including an active role with the St. Vincent de Paul Society. The Corcoran's were married over 50 years at the time she fell victim to the Spanish Influenza epidemic and died in 1919.

Andrew Corcoran died less than 18 months after his wife's passing. An obituary in a local newspaper commented that he had "written his name conspicuously in the history of Jersey City," his death marking the loss of a "truly progressive citizen."

Funeral services for Andrew and Eliza Corcoran took place at St. Aloysius Church and they were laid to rest at Holy Name Cemetery.

Armistice Day to Veterans Day

Like most everyone, I receive a real assortment of emails, many of which go, unopened, straight into the delete folder. I recently received one announcing an upcoming Veterans Day ceremony. Since my husband is a Viet Nam vet, I took a minute to open and read that email. It grabbed my attention by pointing out that the upcoming Veterans Day would fall on the date 11-11-11, a special occasion that would not happen again for a hundred years. A great opening line, it got me thinking and, in a flash, I was in "history detective" mode, searching out the skinny on Veterans Day.

I was vaguely aware that the original name of this holiday of military remembrance was Armistice Day, commemorating the end of World War I. In its day, that war was called the "greatest war in history," although it would lose that distinction two decades later when an even more global conflict, World War II, gripped the world. Although the United States entered World War I in its latter stages as the result of repeated direct provocation by Germany, our national commitment was strong and our sacrifices significant. The signing of the November 11, 1918 armistice agreement that ended active hostilities and set out the framework for post-war Europe was met with great jubilation throughout the country.

Millions of American men were drafted into military service in response to our entry into World War I and thousands of those were from Hudson County. Newspapers routinely reported on Hudson County's draft quotas and the periodic departure of hundreds of local men mustered to meet those quota requirements. These draftees, referred to as war "rookies," were sent off by crowds of cheering and weeping family, friends and neighbors who gathered to wish them well and marching bands that turned out to salute them. Too soon, the rookies would find themselves in trenches in France where close combat, poisonous gas attacks and the spreading influenza epidemic all threatened their survival.

President Woodrow Wilson's armistice announcement meant the end of the draft, victory rallies replacing bittersweet sendoffs and, according to one Hudson newspaper, "wild delirium of joy" erupted at the news of the end of the fighting and the surrender of Germany. The end of World War I was remembered and commemorated each November following the 1918 armistice, even before the designation of Armistice Day as an official holiday.

In the months leading up to the fourth anniversary in 1922, the faithful people of New Jersey were once again coming out in great numbers in support of America's World War I heroes when the repatriated remains of thousands of fallen American soldiers, and some combat nurses, arrived at the Hoboken piers on their way home to their final resting places. Thousands of American families elected to have their loved ones removed from European battlefield cemeteries and returned to the United States. As ships like the transport Wheaton arrived and the caskets of the fallen were off-loaded in Hoboken, local clergy of all faiths collaborated in holding services for the dead on the piers. Each arriving transport ship carried home soldiers from all parts of the country, including local fallen heroes and, with each homecoming, the community came out and came together.

In late 1921, over 1,000 people turned out at the Hoboken piers for services held for 2,400 arriving soldier dead. Earlier that year, President Warren G. Harding, his wife and other dignitaries came to the Hoboken piers to participate in ceremonies when 5,000 soldier dead arrived on the Wheaton.

In the years following the end of World War I, Americans continued to come together to commemorate Armistice Day each November. They did not want to forget the sacrifices of the brave Americans who fought and died for them and they hoped, as does each new generation, that the suffering and painful memories of one war could prevent another.

1906 Disasters & New Jersey Charity

In the aftermath of Superstorm Sandy, at a time of year when the Jersey Shore is normally taking a long winter's nap and the rest of us are hunkered down counting the days until spring, the daily efforts and daunting struggles of recovery and rebuilding go on. The holiday season was anything but "merry" for so many people but acts of random (and not so random) kindness and the continuing charitable generosity of the people of New Jersey said a lot about who we are and the likelihood that we will not lose interest in our neighbors or the challenges they continue to face. In fact, there is a history of New Jersey people rallying to the aid of others stricken by natural disasters.

As we ponder global warming, rising ocean levels, and weather phenomena with names we vaguely (if at all) knew a few years ago including "tsunami" and "derecho," it turns out that multiple tantrums by Mother Nature occurring in a short period of time are not unprecedented. In April 1906, Italian volcano Mount Vesuvius erupted, killing scores of people in Naples just 11 days before the massive San Francisco earthquake killed thousands.

The citizens of Hudson County were quick to respond to both of those tragedies. Local Italian-Americans organized relief collections to provide financial aid to those affected by Vesuvius. A wide array of disaster relief fundraising was mobilized to raise money for the devastated people and institutions of San Francisco.

Mt. Vesuvius Erupting

The ladies of St. Mark's Church, Van Vorst Square, sent the rector of St. Mary's Church in San Francisco, destroyed in the quake, a complete set of vestments embroidered in white and gold thread in a design of roses and vines. These ladies, members of St. Mark's Senior Embroidery Class, had done the stunning handiwork themselves, making their generous gift all the more significant.

At the Park Theatre, Bergen Point, Bayonne, the owner organized entertainment for a performance benefiting earthquake victims. Freeholders and other politicians served as ushers and over $200 was realized for the relief effort. At the Columbian Club in Jersey City, the Knights of Columbus presented an "all-star" vaudeville program including Sheehan's Minstrel Girls and other professional acts to raise funds as well.

San Francisco Earthquake Aftermath

In Hoboken at the Stevens Institute auditorium, a benefit recital drew nearly a full-house of attendees who were entertained by various musical artists including three who called San Francisco their home: sopranos Mrs. Benjamin Lathrop and Miss Lillie Lawlor, and Miss Elizabeth Ames, a cellist. Also performing was Miss Kitty Cheatham, a popular singer remembered for her contributions to children's music and for organizing children's concerts for the N.Y. Philharmonic and other orchestras.

The *Evening Journal* newspaper, in concert with the "Citizens Committee," publicized and encouraged reader donations to a trust fund administered by the Treasurer of the Commercial Trust Company. Just two weeks after the earthquake struck San Francisco, over $9,000 had been contributed to that fund and donor names, large and small, were published in the newspaper, including $25 donations each from Jersey City Mayor Mark Fagan and Oscar Schmidt, the owner of a local musical instrument manufacturing company. The smallest donations were 25 or 50 cents, some of those collected by classes of school children, while among the largest were donations of $125 to $500 collected by employees working at the Andrew J. Corcoran manufacturing company, the James Leo box factory and Mullins & Sons home furnishings.

Speaking as one who bonded and banded together with neighbors in the aftermath of Superstorm Sandy, showering next door where there was hot water and sharing generators via bright orange extension cords that snaked from yard-to-yard, may we keep faith with our fellow New Jersey residents whose losses were so severe and whose problems are far from over.

Arnold Wydeveld & August Will:

New Jersey Artists

In the summer of 2010 we traveled to Ireland where I had arranged for my husband to go salmon fishing on the River Moy while I took watercolor painting lessons. With the Irish instructor's close direction and assistance, two lovely paintings and some very pleasant memories resulted from those lessons while, at the same time, my husband happily bagged two fine Irish salmon. Since the days of cave paintings, humans have used art to tell stories, communicate feelings and memorialize people, places and things.

In the mid-1800s, two men, each an immigrant artist with the initials A.W., settled in New Jersey as new Americans. One was a painter of cityscapes and bucolic local views, capturing the changing community around him for a half-century. The other painted still life, capturing vignettes of ripe peaches, grapes and strawberries posed gracefully on a tabletop or a freshly-caught trout just off the hook.

Arnold Wydeveld was born in Holland in about 1823 and came to America in the early 1850s. A bachelor, he lived on Hudson and Palisade Avenues in Hudson City where he rented rooms that served as his studio and sleeping quarters over the next half-century.

Wydeveld painted still lives of fruit and flowers and fish studies. By the early 1860s his paintings were advertised at New York gallery auctions and were being collected by art connoisseurs such as Henry T. Chapman, Jr. of Brooklyn. His work was exhibited at the National Academy of Design in New York, the Pennsylvania Academy of Fine Arts and the Brooklyn Art Association.

Arnold Wydeveld Still Life Painting

Wydeveld was alternately described as standoffish and peculiar, charming and possessed of a "beautiful character," and mostly a mystery to Hudson County locals. He seemed to have a close friendship with William Peter, the founder of the William Peter

Brewery of Union Hill. Peter was a local artist and perhaps that was the basis of their long relationship. In 1905, at the age of 82, Wydeveld was struck by an express wagon while crossing a street in Lower Manhattan and died three days later at Bellevue Hospital. It was reported that he asked for his friend Peter just before passing away. In fact, it was Peter who made the arrangements for Wydeveld's burial in the Flower Hill Cemetery in North Bergen. Recent auction records for Wydeveld's work show asking prices in the $1,000 to $5,000 range.

August Will was born in Germany in 1834 and, like his contemporary Wydeveld, immigrated to America in the early 1850s. Will married in about 1855 and the couple had six children, not all of them surviving to adulthood. The family lived for many years on Belmont Avenue in Jersey City. Will began sketching views of Jersey City in the 1850s and continued to do so over the next five decades, often returning to a view he had previously drawn to sketch it again. As he rambled and sketched, he saw the growing, changing city and anticipated more of the same in coming years. That prescience resulted in a priceless visual record of Jersey City pre-urbanization and pre-industrialization, done in multiple mediums including watercolor and pen and ink.

August Will

Will also taught art for over thirty years at his New York studio and was an accomplished commercial artist and illustrator whose work appeared in publications such as *Harper's, Scribner's* and *Century Magazine.* An active member of the Arts Club of Jersey City, he loaned his Jersey City images for exhibitions sponsored by that group in 1905, 1906 and 1907, and his work was also exhibited at the National Academy of Design.

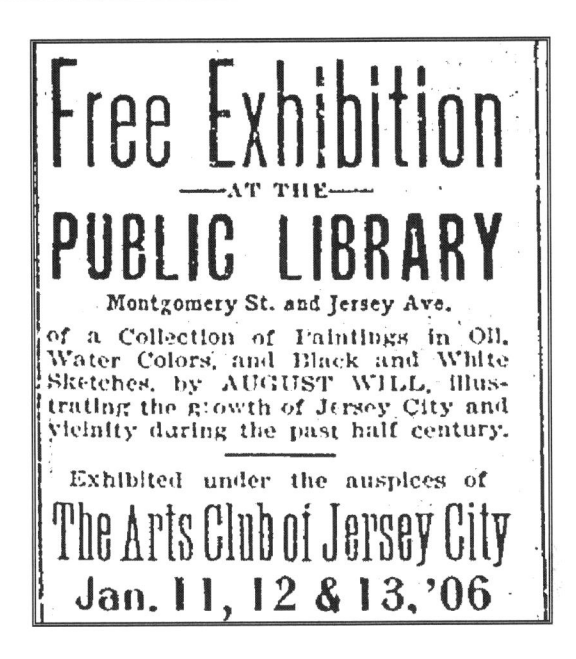

> **Free Exhibition**
> —AT THE—
> **PUBLIC LIBRARY**
> Montgomery St. and Jersey Ave.
>
> of a Collection of Paintings in Oil, Water Colors, and Black and White Sketches, by AUGUST WILL, illustrating the growth of Jersey City and vicinity during the past half century.
>
> Exhibited under the auspices of
> **The Arts Club of Jersey City**
> Jan. 11, 12 & 13, '06

After more than fifty years of capturing scenes of his adopted home, Will died of heart disease in January, 1910 at his Belmont Avenue home and was laid to rest in the New York Bay Cemetery. He left a portfolio of over 100 Jersey City views with instructions that it should only be sold to the City. That happened in 1923 when the Jersey City Public Library acquired the prized collection.

Today, more than a century after Wydeveld and Will made New Jersey their home, local artists and galleries continue to do the same, sharing their work and artistic vision with the communities around them.

Charles Schreyvogel:
Hoboken Painter

For most of us, the biggest downside immediately following Thanksgiving is stepping on the scale and being forced to face up to the result of our overindulgence in the turkey, trimmings and tempting pies that graced our holiday tables. Not so for early 20th century Hoboken artist Charles Schreyvogel, whose ill-fated Thanksgiving meal of 1912 proved deadly when a sliver of poultry bone pierced his gum and ultimately led, some weeks later, to a fatal case of blood poisoning at age 51.

Charles Schreyvogel, born on the East Side of Manhattan in 1861, was the son of Paul Schreyvogel, a German-born confectioner and shopkeeper and his wife Teresa Erbe. In the 1870s, the Schreyvogel family moved to Hoboken where young Charles attended public school and worked as an office boy, apprentice in a pipe-manufacturing company and then as a lithography shop apprentice. Interested in drawing and painting from childhood, Schreyvogel was fortunate to cross paths with H. August Schwabe of the Newark Art League who encouraged him to attend art classes sponsored by that organization. Those classes led to Schreyvogel giving art lessons to supplement the wages he earned working in the lithography shop.

Charles Schreyvogel

In the early 1880s, while living on Hudson Street, Schreyvogel was introduced to Dr. William R. Fisher, an art connoisseur who saw talent in the young artist and recommended that he go to Europe to study art. Schwabe and Fisher provided the financial resources necessary to underwrite Schreyvogel's three years of studies at the Munich Art Academy. After finishing school in Germany, Schreyvogel returned to Hoboken and his work as a lithographer while also painting portraits, miniature paintings on ivory and doing sketchwork for calendar manufacturers. Popular success eluded Schreyvogel despite his formal studies and benefactors.

He established a Hoboken studio and struggled to make a living while trying to promote his work during the 1890s. About that time, good fortune visited Schreyvogel once again when he made an acquaintance with William "Buffalo Bill" Cody that resulted in the opportunity to visit Cody's Wild West Show where he sketched cowboys, Indians and horses. (In a 1900 newspaper interview, Schreyvogel told the reporter that, as a child, he "dreamed" of painting Indians.)

Schreyvogel Painting on Hoboken Rooftop

In 1893 at age 32, three life-changing events took place in Schreyvogel's life: his beloved mother died, he fell in love with Louise Walther of Hoboken and he made his first trip West. He spent several months in Colorado on the Ute Reservation sketching Indian life and then moved on to Arizona where he spent time drawing cowboys.

In August 1894, Schreyvogel and Walther married, reportedly despite her father's objections. Schreyvogel continued working as a lithographer as there was little interest in his Western paintings although he exhibited at the Pennsylvania Academy of Fine Arts in Philadelphia and the National Academy of Design in New York.

All that changed in 1899 when Schreyvogel reluctantly entered his Western painting "My Bunkie" in the annual exhibition of the National Academy of Design and won the highest prize, $300. That same painting, which had at one time hung on consignment in an East Side restaurant to no takers, also won medals at the Paris and Pan-American Expositions and is now in the collection of The Metropolitan Museum of Art. Schreyvogel became a so-called "overnight success" that brought him to the attention of the art community and President Teddy Roosevelt who invited the artist to the White House.

The most accomplished and famous Western artist of that era, Frederic Remington, apparently was unimpressed with Schreyvogel's work which he criticized in newspapers of the day as historically inaccurate. Elizabeth Custer, widow of General George Custer, defended Schreyvogel's work. Schreyvogel reportedly made no direct response to Remington's allegations. Schreyvogel made several additional trips West doing research for his paintings at Indian reservations and Army posts.

With Frederic Remington's death in 1909 from complications resulting from an appendectomy, Schreyvogel became known as the pre-eminent painter of the American West. Notwithstanding such success, a local newspaper reporting Schreyvogel's death three years later stated that the artist "was doing hack work for lithographers in 1900" when his oil painting "My Bunkie" unexpectedly won the prize at the National Academy. *Hack work?* Schreyvogel oil paintings have sold in recent years for over one million dollars.

"My Bunkie"

"Dr." Oliver Phelps Brown:

Herbal "Medicine" Practitioner

After avoiding any need for hospitalization for 25 years, the odds caught up with me a few years ago when I took a fall that broke my kneecap. When I was barely off the crutches after reconstructive knee surgery, my appendix went bad and I was back in a hospital bed. Any nonchalance I had about the quality and cost of healthcare disappeared in short order. These days, the debate over Obamacare, Medicare, and the general future of healthcare in America leaves many of us nursing a headache or an acid stomach. May I prescribe the following story about one Dr. O. Phelps Brown, a mid-1800s Jersey City herbal medicine practitioner, as a temporary diversionary curative?

Oliver Phelps Brown was born in 1824 in Vermont according to the 1860 U.S. census. At the time that census was taken, Brown was recorded as a resident of the First Ward in Jersey City, living and operating his medical enterprise on Grand Street. He told the census-taker his occupation was "patent medicine," and that he owned real estate valued at $18,000 and personal property valued at $3,000. Brown was obviously very well off. The story of how that came to be is a tale of a very clever con man selling snake-oil and false hopes.

Starting in the mid-1850s, first in the Boston area and later in New York and Jersey City, newspapers carried ads for a new miracle cure for consumption, asthma, bronchitis, and other debilitating conditions of the lungs, stomach and nerves. Marketed by a Dr. H. James and called "The Retired Physician's Remedy," advertising stated that the tonic was discovered by the good doctor in Calcutta in a desperate response to his own daughter's life-threatening illness. It was sold as an "East Indian Preparation" containing extract of Cannabis for the price of $2.00 per bottle and available from Dr. James at 19 Grand Street, Jersey City. By 1858, these same advertisements, including heartfelt user testimonials, directed that payment be sent to O.P. Brown, *proprietor* of Dr. H. James Remedies at the same address. It wasn't long before Oliver P. Brown took on the title of "Dr." himself.

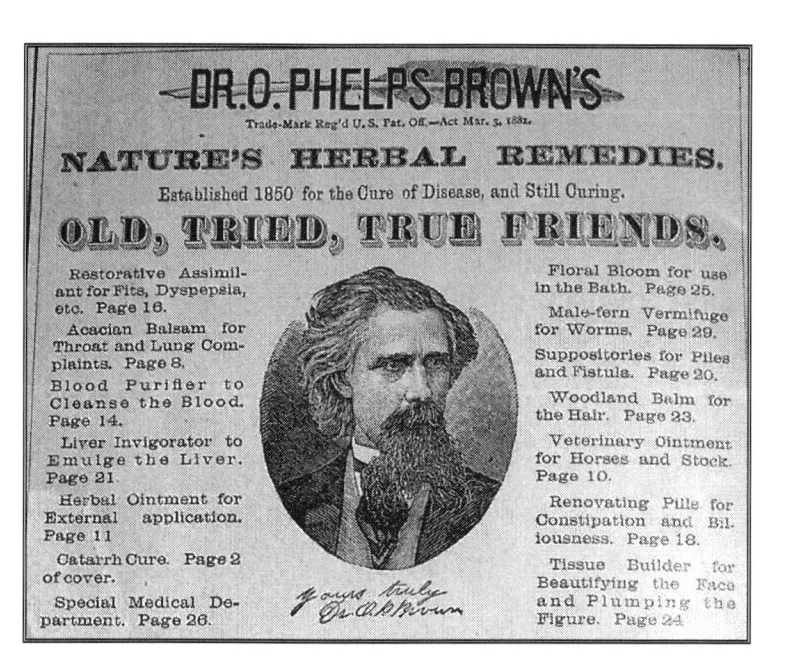

While "Dr." Brown's enterprise was quickly making him a wealthy man, not everyone was taken in. The *New York Leader* newspaper published an exposé of what it characterized as Brown's "medical schemes." According to that paper, Dr. H. James never existed and was an invention of Oliver P. Brown, a failed New England printer who hired an old Jersey City man named Kuyper to play the part of James when needed. As proof of this accusation, the article included the transcript of a letter from then Jersey City Mayor Samuel Westcott stating that "there is no such person as Old Dr. James residing in our city, but an old man is employed to impersonate him and the whole matter is understood here as an imposition."

The exposé went on to say that Brown "traveled in petticoats too," advertising the sale of "The Milk of Roses and Extract of Elder Blossoms" under the pseudonym Madame Julie Melville. This fine product, also $2.00 a bottle, proved to be composed of magnesia and alcohol without a trace of the promised botanical balms. Brown's misdirected enterprising creativity also took the form of Dr. Tracy Delorme, who offered a remedy for "fevers, fits, agues and dyspepsia" discovered by a young girl in a trance-like state.

Despite the efforts of several newspapers around the country that picked up and republished the *New York Leader's* scathing rebuke of Brown as a charlatan preying on "the invalid and ignorant" and an "unprincipled concoctor" akin to a pickpocket or highwayman, the cash continued to roll in. Estimates of his resulting fortune ranged as high as $30,000 and more. Brown would go on to publish a 400-page book in 1867 in Jersey City titled *The Complete Herbalist* and also published his own yearly almanac for many years, maintaining a veneer of respectability despite the accusations against him.

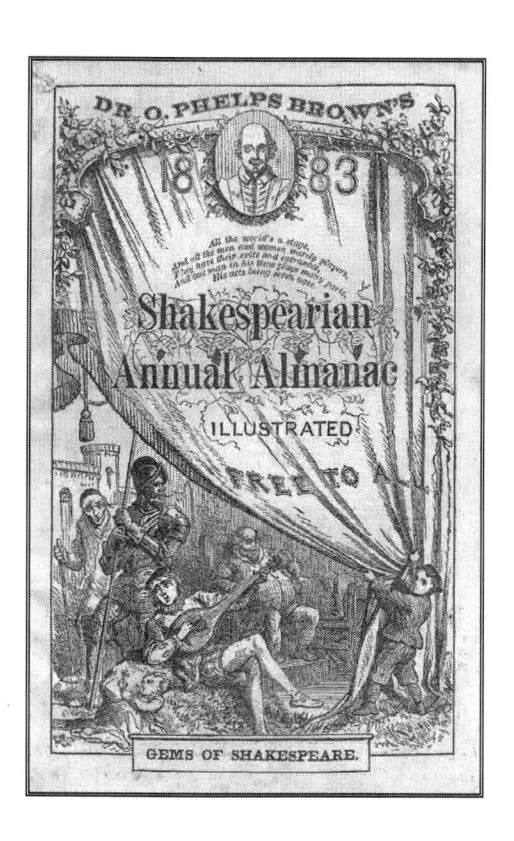

Brown died in Connecticut in November 1878 at age 53 just weeks after a Hudson County newspaper carried an ad offering his "elegant and commodious" house at 48 Grand Street for rent during his planned extended visit to Europe. A Michigan newspaper noted his death saying that the "retired physician" was one O. Phelps Brown, a "tramp printer who hit upon a clever advertising dodge and amassed a fortune," the moral of his life being that "it paid to advertise." As for that miracle cure of his derived from Cannabis extract, it was said to contain no marijuana and was instead a mix of licorice, slippery elm and honey.

Fred Astaire & Young Gus Suckow

Writing a column has led to people sharing their Hudson County connections with me, a happy side effect for someone who never tires of a trip in the "way-back machine." A close friend of 20 years surprised me with the story of her grandfather, an early 1900s child vaudevillian from Bayonne. Research in newspaper archives yielded a number of articles about that young fellow, Gus Suckow, who performed both as a solo act and with his brother Harry. While searching for articles about young Suckow, I spotted a story about another pair of siblings and child vaudevillians of the time, young Fred Astaire and his sister Adele, who were among those performing at the Hudson Theatre in Union Hill during Christmas week, 1909.

Young Performers – Fred & Adele Astaire

Fred and Adele Astaire, who had made their debut performance in Keyport in 1905 when Fred was only six years old, were billed as "popular favorites" and "clever entertainers" in the Hudson Theatre's advertising that also boasted that the theater offered "vaudeville on par with New York." Built at an estimated cost of $125,000, the Hudson opened in September 1905 and was hailed as the first modern theater in the North Hudson section. The builder was a local businessman, Frederick Klein of Jersey City. A principal in an insurance firm by trade, Klein got into the theater business when he acquired the Bon Ton Theatre in a foreclosure only to discover its value as an investment property.

On opening night at the Hudson, politicians and other notables turned out along with a throng of local residents that filled every seat, spilled over into the aisles and reportedly well-exceeded the building's stated capacity of 1,400 people. After the opening show, the Mayor and his retinue celebrated at a champagne supper at George Vix's café. Over the years, the Hudson Theatre would host "high class" vaudeville acts, burlesque follies, acrobats, comedians, plays and even a hypnotist named Pauline who invited the Physicians' Club of North Hudson to attend a "scientific demonstration of the influence of hypnotism on blood pressure." The Hudson eventually came under the umbrella of the Keith theatrical organization, undergoing a renovation and relaunch as part of that franchise.

Hudson Theatre, Union Hill, N. J.

No need for me to recount what happened to Fred Astaire who entertained theatre and movie-goers for decades after that 1909 engagement at the Hudson Theatre. But what about that *local* favorite, Bayonne's Gus Suckow? Born in 1892, his family lived on Avenue "E" and his father was a successful local businessman known around Bayonne as "Wait-A-Minute" Suckow.

Young Suckow's repertoire included singing, acting in sketches, comedy and impersonations, including his specialty, an impersonation of George M. Cohan. His earliest performances were done gratis for various local organizations and events. From that he developed a loyal local following. In 1905, he debuted at the Park Theatre at Bergen Point, Bayonne, to enthusiastic audience response according to a local newspaper. The theatre manager, Mr. Schiller, invited Suckow back for subsequent engagements that were attended by local groups including the Bayonne Democratic Club and the Jersey City Elks, who sent the young performer a congratulatory floral arrangement in the form of a horseshoe measuring six feet high. At the end of Suckow's engagement in the summer of 1906, the Park Theatre's manager presented him with a gold watch.

My friend, Suckow's granddaughter, told me she had a 1905 photo of him decked out with top hat. I had to see it. Being an avid genealogist, I instinctively turned the photo over to see if anyone had recorded the name of the dapper young fellow. It was blank. Handing her a pencil, I suggested that she write down her grandfather's name, year of birth and the names of his children, one of whom was her mother, then in her 80s. Knowing me and my obsession with preserving family history, she dutifully complied. While his theatrical career did not rival that of Fred Astaire, family members say that the style and charisma Suckow displayed as a young entertainer remained with him throughout his life.

Gus Suckow

Halloween in Days Gone By

The record rain of late has reportedly caused some pumpkin shortages in the Northeast. That scarcity may mean that the "jack" in jack-o-lantern will also stand for a corresponding jack-up of prices for the orange orbs of October. But pumpkins alone do not Halloween make. The other essential element is, of course, costumes. Having sons, I never had a frilly (and complicated) princess or ballerina costume to worry about. Instead, I whipped up homemade versions of pirates, Superman, monks, "hobos" and the like. I confess to having dressed up as Raggedy Ann for a party at my sons' school which I am only now thinking might have been a tad embarrassing for them. I still have a photo taken that day, memorializing me in a pinafore and red yarn wig.

Child or adult, the chance to dress-up as a favorite character has a long history of bringing fun and excitement, no matter the age of the masquerader. As early as the 1870s, Halloween parties and socials were hosted by some Hudson fraternal organizations. On Halloween evening, October 31, 1879, an operatic adaptation of Washington Irving's *The Legend of Sleepy Hollow* was presented at the Academy of Music in Jersey City.

Theatre-goers in their finery, strolling down Gregory or York Street would have been wise to keep an eye out for adolescent Halloween pranksters hiding in doorways awaiting the chance to pop out and douse unsuspecting passersby with a blanket of flour.

> **Academy of Music!**
> GREGORY STREET, JERSEY CITY
> E. H. GOUGE................Lessee and Manager.
>
> **TO-NIGHT!**
>
> MAX MARETZEK'S
> HIGHLY SUCCESSFUL ORIGINAL AMERICAN OPERA,
>
> **SLEEPY HOLLOW**

Halloween celebrations remained popular as the 1800s gave way to the 20th century and were all the thing in the years leading up to World War I, particularly for adults. "Society" pages reported on Halloween house parties hosted by the ladies of Hudson County where fortune-telling and other games dabbling in the "black arts" were a favorite with party guests. All things supernatural were possible on Halloween, when otherworldly spirits could commune with earthbound revelers who, for one night, "might do what they would not do at any other time."

In October 1910, the Jersey City Public Library then, as now, a great community resource, put together a history of the origins and customs connected with Halloween including a suggested reading list of books, magazine articles and poetry. The history explained that Halloween, or All Hallows Eve, was a cauldron concoction of ingredients from classic mythology, Druidic and ancient Roman beliefs and Christian superstitions that bubbled up into a potent supernatural stew of spirits and spooks, with more than a dash of romantic spice. Halloween and romance, *really*?

Oh yes. According to the Library, those "must have" Halloween supernatural parlor games mentioned above where fortunes and futures were told, had their origins in some of the earliest Halloween celebration rituals. In their day, those rituals combined spells and ceremonies for divining love connections including predicting the identity of a future spouse or testing the faithfulness of one's partner. Fruit and nuts were often the instruments of divination. Apples were pared and young ladies took turns tossing the peels in the air, sure that when the airborne peels returned to earth, they would take the form of an initial, thus revealing the name of a future mate. I wonder if that would work on *The Bachelorette*.

Over a century ago, in 1911, the following poem, aptly titled *Halloween*, appeared in a Hudson County newspaper and harkened back to those days when Halloween was a day for *romantic* tricks and treats:

"It is the night when goblins stalk
And banshees on the terrace walk;
When sad sepulchered spirits dare
To seek a breath of midnight air.

Through darkened halls when daylight fades
They glide to meet their friendly shades
While pumpkins grin. Oh fearsome sight –
Beware – the ghosties dance tonight.

Within the mirror holding high
A candle - gaze with steady eye;
Observe, above your shoulder peer
The one you'll wed within the year;

And later, in a fateful game,
An apple peel will spell the name
Of one you love. But read aright,
Take care. The spooks are out tonight."

Happy Halloween!

Hoboken:

Home of Competitive Baseball

No sooner have we welcomed a new year when thoughts turn to spring and the opening of the major league baseball season. What a long, colorful road America's favorite pastime has traveled since the days when the first competitive game of baseball was played in Hoboken over 165 years ago.

THE AMERICAN NATIONAL GAME OF BASE BALL.
GRAND MATCH FOR THE CHAMPIONSHIP AT THE ELYSIAN FIELDS, HOBOKEN, N.J.

On that day in June 1846, two clubs, the New Yorks and the Knickerbockers, traveled across the Hudson to battle for the championship of New York in the park-like setting of Hoboken's Elysian Fields. Although the event didn't generate much press interest at the time, it was reported that a "sprinkling of fans" did gather around the field to view the goings-on. The game, won by the New Yorks in a rout, was played under rules drafted by baseball pioneer Alexander Cartwright. While baseball may be the first thing people think of when Elysian Fields is mentioned, its history is, in fact, a story of many years before and after that first baseball battle and a tale of good (and not so good) times there.

The story of Elysian Fields was set in motion in 1811 when Colonel John Stevens III, Revolutionary War veteran, inventor, and

Hoboken's founding father, established the first-ever steam ferry service, the route linking Hoboken and New York City. Over the ensuing years, Elysian Fields became a growing favorite of locals and New Yorkers seeking a pleasure outing. By the early 1830s, the natural beauty of its walkways, green lawns and river views, activities such as cricket and bass fishing, and amenities including picnic grounds attracted visitors of all classes seeking recreational respites.

In 1893, the *New York Herald* ran a lengthy illustrated piece titled "Last of Famous Elysian Fields – The Long Favored Amusement Haunts of New Yorkers Soon to Disappear." The thrust of the article was a nostalgic look back in light of the expected loss of the last vestiges of what was the Elysian Fields resort. Among the sites highlighted, then gone, was the Colonnade Hotel, built in the 1830s and described as having had an "all-white front, Doric pillars and shingled roof" that "pleasantly contrasted with the soft green lawns and rich foliaged trees" around it.

Another was the once nearby Otto Cottage Garden, a favorite of German-Americans who, according to the *Herald*, "tarried there to quaff their beer" and enjoy "their native talent" on an open-air stage, joining in song as performers played "spirited ditties" on zithers and dulcet guitars.

In 1851, forty years before that *Herald* article, the same newspaper reported on another gathering of German-Americans, over 10,000 of them mostly from New York, who had come to Hoboken to celebrate the "May Fest." That celebratory event had descended into mayhem at the Elysian Fields when a melee broke out between attendees and interloping young men belonging to New York gangs known as the "Rock Boys" and "Short Boys." The press reported that gang members had helped themselves to sausages and beer and then took a cigar from a vendor and refused to pay for it, setting off what newspapers around the country headlined as the "Hoboken Riot." Shots were fired, some deaths and many injuries were reported and more than 50 men were arrested.

And then there was Sybil's Cave, a whole story on its own. Much has been written about that attraction, tucked beneath a high rocky cliff at the Elysian Fields, where its spring water once sold for a penny a glass and was touted to have "mysterious and invigorating medicinal qualities." That was before the Board of Health did testing on the water in the 1880s, declaring it unfit for human consumption.

In the summer of 1841, a tragic event forever linked Sybil's Cave and a young woman named Mary Cecilia Rogers. Mary, about 20 years old and said to be an exceptional beauty, lived in New York City with her widowed mother and worked as a salesgirl in a cigar shop. On July 25th, Mary left her home saying she was going to visit a relative in Manhattan. She never made it there and never returned home. Several days later, her battered body was found floating in the Hudson River, just offshore, at Sybil's Cave.

Every lurid detail of her death including graphic descriptions of her body and rumors about her personal life were splashed across the pages of newspapers across the country. Less than three months after the discovery of her body, Mary's fiancé traveled from New York to Hoboken where, drunk and despondent, he reportedly took poison and killed himself at Sybil's Cave, near the very spot where Mary's lifeless body had lain. The murder case was never solved but was memorialized by Edgar Allen Poe in his detective tale *The Mystery of Marie Roget*.

Early Image of Sybil's Cave

Hot Air Ballooning in New Jersey

The passing of Dr. Sally Ride, America's first woman in space, got me thinking about the ages-old human fascination with the heavens above and beyond this planet we call home. Greek mythology gave us the tale of Icarus who donned prosthetic wax wings that melted when he flew too close to the sun. Over 500 years ago, artistic genius and inventor Leonardo Da Vinci drew amazing detailed sketches of flying machines and parachutes. Just a century ago, the Wright Brothers launched the modern age of aeronautics. Only a scant few decades after their very brief flights at Kitty Hawk, air travel would become a normal mode of transportation and plans were in motion to send men - and women - into space.

In between the days of Da Vinci and the Wright Brothers, New Jersey played host to another aeronautical achievement in 1819 when a French balloonist lifted off near Paulus Hook in Jersey City and, at an altitude of some 500 feet, cut his basket loose and parachuted in it to the ground. The basket fell some 200 feet before the parachute opened, giving the assembled crowd of about 3,000 spectators both a thrill and a fright. The daredevil, Louis Charles Guille, landed safely near the spot from where he had ascended and is credited with having made the first parachute jump in the western world that November day.

> Monsieur Guille made a second ascent in a Balloon from Powles' Hook, near New-York, on Saturday last. He descended in the car from a height of 500 feet, without injury, and alighted about 150 yards from the place where he ascended.

In his haste to cut the ropes holding the balloon to the basket, Guille cut into his thigh, that being his only injury. The balloon, once freed from the basket, passed high over the city heading in the direction of Long Island. Guille would go on to do similar events in the Northeast and was sued for damages when one of his wayward balloons came down in a New England garden.

Seventy-five years after Guille stunned the crowd at Paulus Hook, New Jersey had its own home-grown balloonist daredevil, twenty-year-old Agnes Grace Stage who performed under the name Nina Madison. "Nina," born in Brooklyn in 1875, grew up on New York Avenue in Jersey City where her family relocated in the late 1870s and was described as "modest," a "pleasing conversationalist," and having "her share of good looks." She created quite a sensation in May 1895 in Bayonne when 10,000 people watched her, smartly dressed in a navy blue suit, hanging from a trapeze bar affixed to a hot air balloon. As the balloon ascended, it grazed the roof of a nearby hotel, causing her terrified mother to faint below. Upon reaching a height where she appeared not more than a dark speck in the sky, Nina deployed an umbrella-like parachute and began a fairly rapid descent into a grove of trees in Greenville. Tangled in a tree but unhurt, she was helped down by some locals enjoying a picnic nearby. A horse-drawn carriage transported her back to the point of liftoff, much to the relief and delight of the anxious crowd.

AMUSEMENTS.

Arlington Park
Boulevard and 51st St., Bayonne.
GRAND BALLOON ASCENSION
And PARACHUTE LEAP
Every Saturday and Sunday Afternoon
at 3:30 o'clock, by Miss NINA MADISON, Champion Lady Aeronaut of the World. Grand Concerts by Prof. Seifert's Celebrated Band.
ADMISSION FREE.   aug5 f&s t sep1 1p

So, what on earth (or in heaven) prompted a Jersey girl of the late 19th century to want to be an aeronaut? Nina had been at the Eldorado in Weehawken where she saw "Professor" Leo Stevens performing balloon ascensions. Immediately hooked, she sought Stevens out and became his protégé. By the time she entertained those 10,000 spectators in Bayonne, she had made several hundred balloon ascensions in the U.S., Canada and South America, the highest of those reaching an altitude of 10,000 feet.

Just two months after her triumph in Bayonne, the odds caught up with Nina when she was performing at Haverhill, Massachusetts. Strong winds caused the balloon to rip while in flight with Nina in tow. The balloon began a very fast descent from about 200 feet landing in a stand of pine trees. Nina scraped her back and sprained her ankle but, amazingly, broke no bones, perhaps owing to the fact that she reportedly fainted during the fall to earth. The first telegraphic reports of the incident stated that the young balloonist and parachutist had been tragically killed in the incident. Those reports were soon retracted and, shortly after, Miss Madison returned to New York Avenue for a visit with her parents where she rested her injured ankle before leaving for a series of engagements in Canada.

Spanish Influenza Epidemic

When I was five years old, we moved from Jersey City to Union Beach, a place where my parents could afford to purchase a small ranch house with carport. For many years after, I spent two to three weeks each summer back in Jersey City, visiting my maternal grandparents at their apartment on Rose Avenue in Greenville. I loved staying with them and being the center of my grandmother's attention. My grandparents never owned a car so my grandmother and I would take the bus to Journal Square to shop or see a movie.

One summer I unexpectedly came down sick, very sick. My grandmother tucked me in up to my chin in her own bed and called for the family's faithful physician, Dr. Front. He was what used to be called a (very) "tall drink of water," and had to duck his head when coming through the doorways of the apartment. When he appeared at my bedside, I am told that my eyes opened wide like saucers. No doubt. Looking up from my sickbed to take in the whole of him was quite an experience. His diagnosis: the grippe. Today, the word grippe, coming from a French word meaning "seize suddenly," has been replaced by the modern term "influenza," the two words being essentially synonymous. For decades before that summer I took sick in Jersey City, New Jersey residents had been stricken by periodic grippe outbreaks including in 1889 and 1892.

The most serious of those was the 1918 "Spanish" influenza pandemic that first broke out in Europe and killed thousands of soldiers on the battlefields of World War I before making its way to the United States. The first reports of suspected Spanish flu cases in Hudson County occurred in September, 1918. Over the next month, newspapers carried daily counts of new cases, those numbers sometimes reaching 200 or more in a single day in Jersey City alone. In early October, a local newspaper reported the tragic story of the Kelly family who lived on Grove Street in downtown Jersey City. Mr. Kelly, an inspector with an express company and the brother of two soldiers serving in France, died after contracting the flu. As Kelly's mortal remains awaited religious services at St. Mary's R.C. Church and burial at Holy Name Cemetery, his pregnant wife, also infected and near death, gave birth to a baby that died shortly thereafter. There was an outpouring of grief in Jersey City and Mayor Frank Hague and other community officials attended Tom Kelly's funeral.

The same week that Tom Kelly died, an urgent call was made for "patriotic" women to volunteer to make gauze masks under the auspices of the Greenville Red Cross on Linden Avenue. As the new cases mounted, flu deaths were listed in local newspapers and in Bayonne and Jersey City, hard-hit by the outbreak, the Boards of Health mandated that schools, saloons, ice cream parlors, churches, pool rooms and other public gathering places close until further notice.

Hospitals and doctors were overwhelmed by the sick and dying. Local undertakers were unable to obtain sufficient numbers of coffins for the dead and there were fears about possible contamination as the result of delayed burials. The New York Bay Cemetery stopped interring the dead due to not having enough gravediggers to open the graves and bodies were temporarily stored in vaults where possible. In the middle of this crisis, local liquor dealers organized an angry demonstration in Jersey City and, in response, Mayor Hague agreed to reopen saloons, a decision that was roundly criticized by health officials.

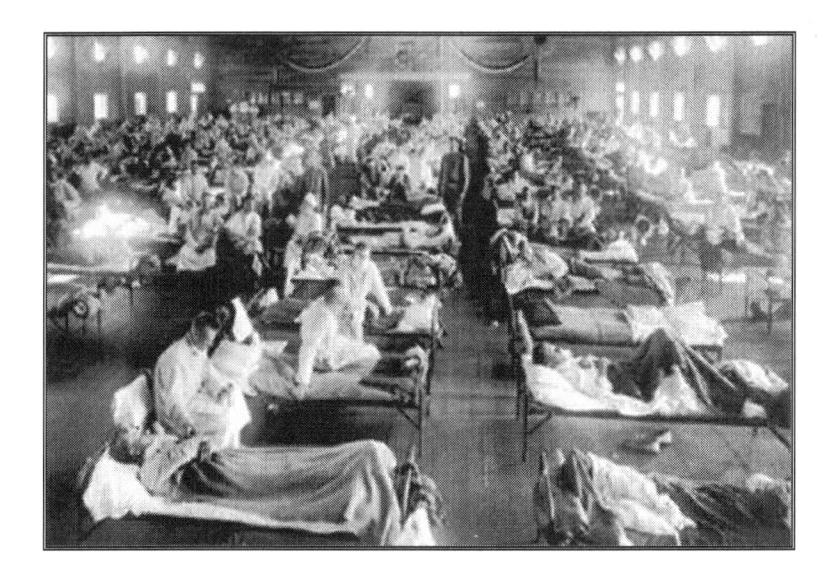

The Spanish flu struck millions of people around the world and at every level of society, from European royalty to the very poor, young and old alike. In Hudson County, one of those who lost his life during the outbreak in October 1918 was a popular local lightweight wrestler known as Young Bon Ton. "Bon Ton," then 29 years old, had been wrestling locally and around the U.S. for several years and had claimed the title "lightweight champion of the world" for himself after he defeated a Canadian wrestler in 1914. When he succumbed to the flu, one of his friends was quoted as saying that Bon Ton had "tried hard to put the full Nelson on the influenza, but failed."

Julius Fehr:
Hoboken Doctor & Inventor

Like many thousands of their fellow residents in the early to mid-20th century, generations of my New Jersey family worked for large local manufacturing companies. My dear grandfather, born in 1900 in Jersey City to my German-born great-grandparents, worked for decades at the Colgate Palmolive factory, retiring from there in the 1960s. I remember standing on the corner of Rose and McAdoo Avenues anxiously waiting for him to come home. My grandparents never owned a car so my grandfather got to and from the Colgate factory by bus and leg-power. Of course, we loyally used Colgate products in our homes including Colgate toothpaste and Cashmere Bouquet powders. I expect my grandfather never knew that, a half century before he was hired by Colgate, another German immigrant, Julius Fehr of Hoboken, received multiple patents for improvements in "deodorizing, antiseptic powders" and "medical compounds and powders for infants."

Julius Fehr, born in 1825, was educated in Darmstedt, Germany where he was apprenticed to a druggist and learned the trade he would practice for the majority of his life. He immigrated to New York in the early 1850s and soon got a job in a pharmacy there.

Several years later, Fehr moved to Hoboken, working in a local pharmacy and eventually taking ownership of that business, located on Washington Street. While working as a druggist, Fehr enrolled in the medical school at the College of Physicians and Surgeons at Columbia University, graduating in about 1869.

Julius Fehr

Probably owing to his years spent as a druggist and his interest in pharmacological science, Fehr did not become a practicing community physician. Instead, in the 1870s, he was engaged in experimentation with magnesium silicate, better known as "talc." Talc, a very soft mineral, is the basic ingredient in what we know as talcum powder, a product used as a moisture barrier in reducing rashes, chafing and other skin irritations. Fehr received U.S. patents in 1873 and 1875 related to his talcum powder compounds.

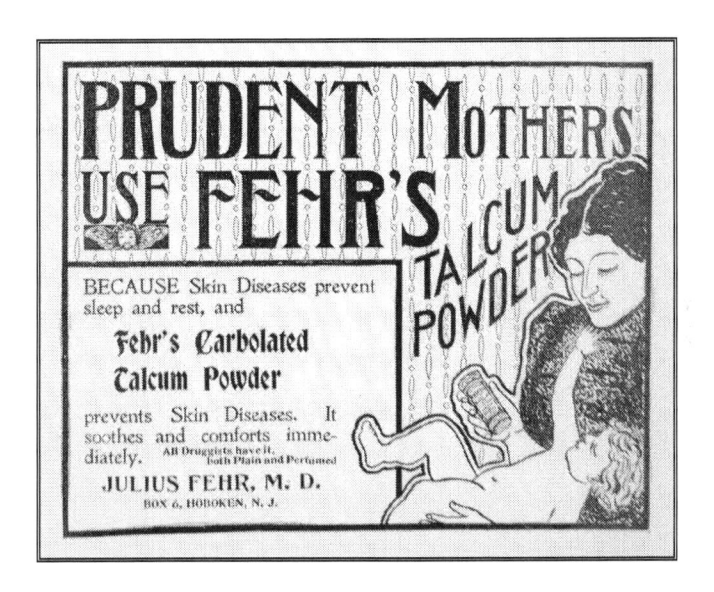

PRUDENT MOTHERS USE FEHR'S TALCUM POWDER

BECAUSE Skin Diseases prevent sleep and rest, and

Fehr's Carbolated Calcum Powder

prevents Skin Diseases. It soothes and comforts immediately. All Druggists have it, both Plain and Perfumed

JULIUS FEHR, M. D.
BOX 6, HOBOKEN, N. J.

In his 1873 patent application, Fehr stated that he had "invented a new and improved Medical Compound . . . made of silicate of magnesia (one thousand parts), carbolic acid (one part) and zinc oxide (one-fifth part)" but capable of being "altered as dictated by the nature and complaint of the user." He also stated that application of his compound to "the sensitive parts of the human body" would keep those body parts "pure and free from putrefaction." In 1875, Fehr filed another patent application due to formula changes and improvements to his original talcum compound. He also expanded the list of uses for the powder to include "soothing" skin irritation due to chafing, scalds and burns and as a baby powder, tooth powder and "for the purpose of drying ladies' hair," stating that the powder could be used "either plain or perfumed, to suit the taste of consumers."

Fehr's talcum powder proved very popular and was recognized by exhibition in conjunction with the American Pharmaceutical Association and at the Philadelphia Centennial Exposition of 1876. Dr. Fehr was a founding member and officer of the N.J. Pharmaceutical Association.

Julius Fehr Laboratory

Scientist and doctor notwithstanding, Fehr was still a businessman. In 1878, a Jersey City newspaper reported that Fehr had been arrested after an incident at his building on Washington Street in Hoboken. Fehr had apparently ceased his pharmacy operation there and, thinking well of his clerk Adolph Flake, had leased the store to Flake even giving him the existing store stock. A subsequent falling out between the two men had culminated in Fehr showing up at the store where, according to the newspaper, he gave Flake "a severe drubbing." Soon remorseful, Fehr was released on a minimal amount of bail.

Fehr's second wife, Antonia, was no less passionate when it came to "negotiation." In 1896, when trolley poles were being erected in Hoboken, a post hole was dug in front of the Fehr residence at 158

Second Street. Mrs. Fehr confronted the workers from the Jersey City, Hoboken & Rutherford Railroad Company, stepping into the hole to make her point. Threats of arrest did not move her. Was she attempting to derail the trolley project? Not really. While standing in the hole, she exclaimed that the railroad had paid her neighbor $150 as compensation for the trolley pole installed in front of their home. "Why can't I get some money?" she bellowed. Police Officer Hildemann, out of options, lifted Mrs. Fehr up and out of the hole and, in response, she told him she would see to it that her husband no longer used Hildemann's brother to ship his merchandise, telling the officer that he would "repent" of what he had done to her.

Karl Bitter:

Weehawken Sculptor

Customarily, the July 4th holiday arrives with a blast of heat, blazing grills and fireworks lighting up the night skies with explosive rainbows of color as we mark the anniversary of our American independence. Tom Jefferson, the author of the Declaration of Independence would no doubt be pleased to see that we continue to celebrate his work and the founding principles of our nation that are as relevant today as they were over two centuries ago when he put his pen to paper.

Jefferson's life and legacy are preserved and remembered across our nation. He looks down on us from Mount Rushmore, we feel his spirit at his stately Virginia home, Monticello, and can enjoy the tranquility of the Jefferson Memorial on the Tidal Basin in Washington. Statues of Jefferson abound, including three that were the work of a Weehawken sculptor, Karl Bitter.

Bitter was born in Austria in 1867 where, as a young man, he trained to be a sculptor at the Vienna Academy of Fine Arts. In 1889, he sailed alone for the U.S. on the S.S. Lahn out of Bremen, Germany, landing in Lower Manhattan and entering the country through the Castle Garden immigration station. Bitter began his new life like so many before and after him, with little money and the enduring immigrant dream of a better future. His artistic training helped him quickly find employment as a skilled laborer working for an architectural decorating firm during which time he crossed paths with noted architect Richard Morris Hunt who recognized Bitter's talent and proved to be a continuing source of encouragement to him.

At the age of 22, when he was working at the architectural decorating company, Bitter entered a competition seeking designs for massive bronze doors to be installed at Trinity Church in Manhattan. Young Bitter's fellow employees reportedly mocked his bravado in submitting his design only to see him win the coveted assignment over many notable and more experienced sculptors of the day. He used his earnings from that project to launch his own studio and, within just ten years of his arrival from Austria, he was a successful, respected artisan and much in demand.

Trinity Church Doors

In 1893, Bitter worked on the architectural sculpture for the Chicago World's Fair and went on to serve as the director for sculpture at the Pan-American Exposition in Buffalo in 1901. Bitter established a residence and studio on the Boulevard in Weehawken in the late 1800s. Perched high on a cliff, the unusual dwelling was one of the largest in North Hudson and was surrounded by a tall stone wall adorned with cherubs and medallions. Bitter was the head of sculpture programs at the St. Louis Exposition in 1904 and was selected to serve as president of the National Sculpture Society.

Karl Bitter

Bitter's works can be found at the 30th Street Station in Philadelphia, the County Courthouse in Cleveland, the Wisconsin State Capitol, the University of Virginia, the University of Michigan, Cornell University, and include many stately public fountains, among those the Pulitzer Fountain in New York City. In addition, Bitter was retained by some of America's wealthiest families including the Vanderbilts. For the Vanderbilt estate, Biltmore, Bitter created magnificent figures of St. Louis the King and Joan of Arc, the Maid of Orleans.

In 1902, Bitter had a brush with death while riding in a coach when the horse was spooked and the driver lost control. Bitter and the coachman were not seriously injured but the newspapers described the coach as having been "kicked to pieces." In April 1915, Bitter was not so lucky when he and his wife were struck by an automobile that jumped the curb and hit them as they were leaving the Metropolitan Opera House shortly before midnight. It was reported that Bitter pushed his wife away from the path of the oncoming car. She survived her injuries but Bitter did not, dying at New York Hospital the following morning at age 47.

Bitter's brilliant career was cut short and we can only imagine what his body of work would have been had he lived. Local newspapers said that Bitter took an "active interest" in the civic affairs in Weehawken. In 1906, one of those publications summed it up as follows:

"In these days when civic beauty is an attainment so greatly to be desired, the presence of a man of Mr. Bitter's artistic ability in a community like Weehawken may do much to lend to the town artistic features that it would not otherwise possess."

Less than six months after Karl Bitter's untimely death, his stunning home on the Boulevard was gutted by a fire that destroyed many valuable and irreplaceable works of art. Fortunately, Mrs. Bitter was not at the house at the time of the fire.

Karl Bitter's Weehawken Home

Lady Liberty

On a lovely end-of-summer day as I cruised up the Turnpike heading for Exit 14C and downtown Jersey City, I caught a glimpse of Lady Liberty in the distance . . . or as I like to call her, America's most well-known immigrant. Measuring over 150 feet tall (base to torch, not including pedestal beneath) and weighing 225 tons, her famous green-patinated copper skin is less than the thickness of two pennies. The iconic lady in the harbor has logged over 125 years of faithful service to our country.

The idea for the creation of a monument to commemorate the achievement of American independence and the alliance between France and the United States was put forth in France as early as the 1860s. French political instability and financial issues delayed action until the 1870s when French sculptor Frederic Auguste Bartholdi was commissioned for the project. Financing continued to be a problem and, in response, the project became a joint effort between France and the United States with fund-raising activities taking place on both continents. It was agreed that our country would be responsible for the building of the pedestal for the statue and France was to be responsible for the creation of the statute, its transportation to America and assembly on-site. It is estimated that over 120,000 Americans contributed to the cause, many of them giving a dollar or less in response to aggressive publicity by publisher Joseph Pulitzer.

Bartholdi

Bartholdi completed the statue's head and the arm holding the torch before he had finished the design for the full statue. The arm with torch was displayed at the 1876 U.S. Centennial Exposition in Philadelphia. The full design received a U.S patent in 1879. With the enormous size and scale of the statue, Bartholdi needed the assistance of an engineer to design the structural framework underneath. Alexandre Gustave Eiffel, the designer of the Eiffel Tower in Paris, took on that role. When completed, the statue was transported to the U.S. in 350 pieces that were reassembled on the newly-constructed pedestal over a 4-month period.

On October 28, 1886, President Grover Cleveland presided over the dedication of the Statue of Liberty. One of the groups participating in the celebratory ticker tape parade in New York and unveiling ceremonies on Bedloe's Island was The Liberty Guards of Jersey City Heights, a local French military and benevolent association. Some months earlier, that organization had honored Frederic Bartholdi by electing him their honorary president. The sculptor responded by letter, graciously thanking the group for the honor bestowed on him, enclosing a photograph of himself, and indicating that he would try to visit with them when next in America.

It was estimated that over 2 million people witnessed the spectacle of the first illumination of the Statue of Liberty and accompanying fireworks display on the evening of the 28th. A Hudson County newspaper reported that "from Guttenberg to Bergen Point, every point of advantage was occupied" including housetops, bluffs and the shoreline. Some 1,500 people gathered on a hill north of Montgomery Street in Jersey City. At the City Hospital, local officials sat on the balcony where they had an excellent view of the bay and fireworks. The roads around the Communipaw shore were packed with people. Many homes were decorated with both American and French flags for the occasion and their stoops were full of excited residents. A cannon salute was fired at the Jersey City Yacht Club and crowds even gathered on the grounds of the New York Bay Cemetery in Greenville. Beyond local residents, hundreds more people came in from other locales on the railroad and city horse-cars were jammed with people determined not to miss the spectacle of a lifetime.

Lady Liberty stood quietly by, a shadowy figure in the dark of the evening. When the carefully choreographed illumination of the torch suddenly lit up the night sky, spectators erupted amid the roar of the horns of hundreds of boats ringing the statue. Spectacular fireworks displays on Bedloe's and Governor's Island and at the Battery launched hundreds of colorful rockets that created images of the "stars and stripes" and the French tricolor flag, thrilling the assembled crowds.

Since then, on a daily basis and without any theatrics or fireworks, the Statue of Liberty has continued to inspire, thrill and create wide-eyed wonder as she greets immigrants from every corner of the world or welcomes Americans home from their travels.

Loewus Brothers:
Liquor Distributors

Over the years, I've heard any number of men, including my husband, describe the benefits and healthful effects of drinking beer. Just this past week, my husband shared a printout of "The Buffalo Theory" with me. That piece of wisdom, attributed to the TV show "Cheers" and a conversation between bar regulars Cliff and Norm, equates survival of the fittest in buffalo herds to a similar process whereby beer drinking results in the death of one's weakest brain cells, thus leaving the drinker with a more fit mind as a happy side effect of imbibing.

Long before Cliff and Norm entertained us on the small screen, Hudson County liquor distributors had advertised the important health effects to be derived from beer, especially for women. In 1911, a local liquor distribution company ran an ad in a Hudson County newspaper titled "The Hand that Rocks the Cradle Rules the World," featuring the image of a young mother gazing lovingly on her infant as she rocks the baby in a wicker cradle. The caption stated the following:

"The ever increasing strength and power of our Great American Nation depends largely on the physical condition of our children. Not only the strength, but also the very life of the child depends upon its proper nourishment in infancy. Good, pure, clean beer more fully supplies just the correct nourishment - in every sense of the word – that mothers require."

"The Hand that Rocks the Cradle Rules the World"

The ever increasing strength and power of our Great American Nation depends largely upon the physical condition of our children. Not only the strength, but also the very life of the child depends upon its proper nourishment in infancy.

Good, pure, clean beer more fully supplies just the correct nourishment in every sense of the word—that mothers require.

PETER DOELGER
FIRST PRIZE BOTTLED BEER
EXPRESSLY FOR THE HOME

Is the one beer that can be absolutely relied upon as being perfectly pure, clean and nutritious. No mother could prepare food with more care than that used in the brewing and bottling of PETER Doelger First Prize Bottled Beer.

$1.25 the case of 24 bottles—one cent a bottle more than the ordinary beer. A little higher in price – a great deal higher in quality.

FOR SALE BY:
| Loewus Bros. & Co., | Flegenheimer Bros., |
| 84 Montgomery Street, Jersey City, N.J. | 176 Newark Avenue, Jersey City, N.J. |

In the early days of the 20th century just before the dark clouds of Prohibition blew in, Hudson County was home to multiple thriving wholesale liquor houses. Among those were the Hoboken firms of Wachtel & Muller, Charles F. Kaegbehn, Paul Seglie, and Italian-born Angelo Podesta who established his liquor business in 1876. Union Hill was home to the liquor house of German-born H.F. Drewes who first trained in the spirits business in his native land at the age of 14 and whose enterprise also included four retail locations in Union Hill and Jersey City. Jersey City was the location for Krause & Co., Michael B. Holmes & Co., McArdle & Co., Lewis Fischer & Brother and Loewus Brothers & Co., the most prosperous of all the competing liquor houses, headquartered at 84 Montgomery Street with retail locations in Jersey City and Bayonne.

Loewus Brothers, established in 1890, was not one of the oldest firms of its kind in Hudson County but it was the most successful when it came to the measure that counted: sales. Gustave and Charles Loewus, the firm's founders, were born in Bohemia and came to America in their late teens, each getting some early experience by working in liquor houses in New York before launching their own company. Their product line included beer, ale, California wines, cordials, whiskeys, champagnes, sherries, and ports sold to saloons, hotels, druggists, grocers and private individuals. It was said that in the 20 years between 1890 and 1910, the company's sales increased with each successive year.

The Loewus brothers were described as being among the smartest businessmen in Hudson County, expert in the selection of staff, trusted and admired for their character, business acumen and "logical minds," and known for a directness and "absence of sentiment" in their business dealings. Case in point: In 1910, when the financially-troubled Bayonne Opera House failed to pay a $300 bill for liquor provided to its café by Loewus Brothers, the brothers quickly retained a local law firm and took legal action against the Bayonne Amusement Company, the owner of the Opera House.

> **LOEWUS BROTHERS' EMPLOYES' FINE OUTING**
>
> Fifty prominent merchants and residents of the Bergen section had an enjoyable time last evening on the annual outing of the Loewus Brothers' Company Employes' Association, which was held at Herig's Newark Bay Shore House, foot of Danforth Avenue. A large trolley car, brilliantly illuminated left the terminal at Bergen Avenue and Montgomery Street at 8:30 o'clock. The party alighted at Danforth and Ocean avenues and enjoyed a shore dinner, which was served in excellent style by Capt. Steve Herig. A stag entertainment concluded the evening's pleasure.

In 1914, a newspaper article reported that Hudson County would have strong representation at the Liquor Dealers State Convention to be held in Atlantic City. Among the notables from Hudson County was Charles Loewus, president of the Wholesale Liquor Dealers' Association of New Jersey. Whether by design or not, the article immediately above that reported on the upcoming "aggressive campaign" planned by the Anti-Saloon Party and local Prohibitionists, including charges that Hudson County officials routinely ignored numerous complaints about chronic violations of existing liquor laws. The struggle over alcohol was heating up and the dry days were on the horizon.

Mother's Day

Mother's Day is the day when we remember and honor the singular selflessness of the women who nurtured and loved us in our earliest days and formative years, whether they were our birth mothers, adoptive mothers or others like grandmothers or aunts who filled that role. The idea for an annual Mother's Day celebration originated with Philadelphian Anna Jarvis who lost her own mother in 1905 and resolved to campaign for the establishment of a national day honoring the sacrifices and contributions of mothers. Her passion and tireless promotion of that idea gave rise to national and international interest and Mother's Day was born soon after.

Anna Jarvis

In those early days, it was local churches that embraced the new Mother's Day celebration and gave it a welcome home. Each year, New Jersey newspapers listed all the local Mother's Day services along with essays, poems, quotations and new "traditions" accompanying the commemoration including the wearing of a white carnation to show maternal devotion. What was sensitively, sensibly and eloquently written then remains just as timely a century later and is worth revisiting as we honor motherhood:

"Mother's Day is to be observed in sermon and song and the pastors will take for their topics the influence of motherhood. All who attend any of the services are asked to wear a white carnation to show their interest and devotion. Later in the day a committee will take some of these flowers to a number of the sick and aged mothers that they too may have part in the observances of the day."

"The white carnation is the official flower of Mother's Day. It's whiteness representing purity; its form, beauty; its fragrance, love; its wide field of growth, charity."

"You are asked to remember with flowers and comforts and a letter of cheer the shut-ins in homes, hospitals and prisons. Such remembrance may set the blood to tingling in the veins of those you may think have no heart and who may think you have none."

"As to ways of observing the day outside of religious exercises, we are urged to honor our mothers by doing some distinct act of kindness and living on that day as our mother would have us do."

"Millions of Americans will wear a white carnation in honor of one of the greatest forces for good that ever came into this sordid world – mother love. No pen can do justice to what mother love has meant to man through all the ages. Were the world tomorrow to go to chaos and despair, mother love would bring it back patiently to sanity and repentance. No sacrifice is too great for mother love to make freely and without complaint. For mother love is the one thing that time cannot change or wither. It is eternal."

"Every day should be Mother's Day. It is a big and beautiful thought, the setting aside of one day in the year when the mother shall hold court in her home or the tender memories of those who have died shall spring fresh into the minds and hearts of the sons and daughters left without her tender care. But, after all, that is only one day – how about the other 364? We are very prone, all of us, to forget the little courtesies and confidences that mean so much to the older folk. We are often intolerant of what we call their 'old-fashioned' ideas and it is not until the whole world sends ringing towards heaven its song of praise of all mothers that we stop and remember and add our voices to that vast chorus. Every day should be Mother's Day (and Father's Day too) and every thrill of love that we feel as we bend over the cribs where our own little ones are sleeping should find an answering note of understanding of the love and patience which guarded our own youthful years."

MOTHER'S DAY—THEN AND NOW

New Jersey Wheelmen

Every January 1st, millions of Americans make New Year's resolutions, promising to change themselves or their lives for the better. By late January, many of us have already fallen off the self-improvement wagon or are hanging on by our white-knuckled fingers. A favorite resolution is to "get more exercise." We buy gym memberships or home exercise equipment, marching for miles on treadmills and cycling to nowhere on stationary bikes. In the late 19th century, adult bicycle riding and racing were hugely popular sporting activities that spawned a different kind of membership - in cycling clubs. Local newspapers had regular "wheelmen" columns that reported on events and competition results and top cyclists became celebrity athletes of the day.

In the 1890s, Hudson County had a long list of bicycling clubs with a reported membership of over 500 wheelmen (and women). Local cycling clubs included the High Grade Wheelmen of West New York, Guttenberg Wheelmen, Niantic Wheelmen of Jersey City, Castle Point Wheelmen of Hoboken, Clio Wheelmen, Arcanum Wheelmen, Lafayette Wheelmen, North Hudson Wheelmen of Union Hill, Catholic Club Cyclers and the Hudson County Wheelmen. Competition among the various local clubs and others from neighboring locales including New York was keen and spirited. One cycling race in July 1897 drew 25,000 spectators who lined four miles of the Boulevard in North Bergen.

One of the standouts among Hudson County cycling racers was William L. Darmer of Jersey City. Darmer, born in the early 1870s, lost his father shortly after that and was raised by his widowed mother Johanna, a local merchant who operated a confectionary shop on Bergen Avenue for many years. In 1892, at age 20, Darmer was a member of the West Bergen Athletic Association and represented Hudson County in a novice class race held at Madison Square Garden. Two months later, at the Belleville Avenue Rink in Newark, Darmer accepted a challenge from a Newark cyclist and rode a borrowed bike to victory in a one-mile race on the inside track. Over the next few years, Darmer went on to be a champion racer with the Hudson County Wheelmen, winning more than 25 competition medals.

WILLIAM L. DARMER.

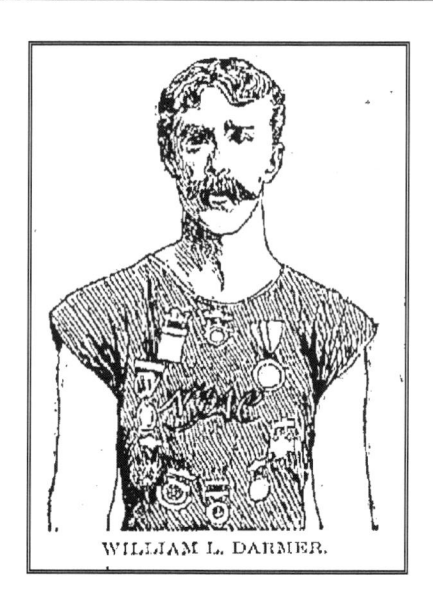

He married the former Sarah Van Nostrand and both husband and wife were active in cycling circles. Sarah Darmer was elected Jersey City consul for the League of American Wheelmen in recognition of her participation in cycling and efforts to recruit other women to the sport. The duties of a consul included looking after "the comfort and welfare of strangers belonging to the League" that were injured in cycling accidents in the consul's jurisdiction. Political correctness not being an issue in newspapers of that era, the press described Sarah as "a bright, young woman and attractive blonde of slender, graceful proportions" attired in "a neat brown bicycle suit with divided skirt, bloomers and leggings," matching "Tam o'Shanter cap," and sporting a "pretty gold badge" with the words "Consul, New Jersey Division LAW." In June 1896, both Darmers were among 98 cyclists riding in a 100-mile "century run" from Jersey

City to Lake Hopatcong and back again, Sarah being one of three women who finished the challenging recreational ride.

Sarah Van Nostrand Darmer

William Darmer teamed up with local track and field athletes to represent the New Jersey Athletic Club in the Metropolitan district A.A.U. championships in a battle against its rival, the Knickerbocker Athletic Club of New York. He was also a soldier in the New Jersey National Guard Hospital and Ambulance Corps and once cycled from Jersey City to a military camp in Sea Girt in a courier race, carrying a message from the Jersey City Mayor Edward Hoos to a Brigadier General.

In between all the above, in late 1894, Darmer had an unplanned cycling adventure. He stopped in to visit his mother at her candy store and interrupted a thief whose hands were literally in the store till. The thief bolted, only to be followed by Darmer who jumped on his bike and pursued the man through the nearby Jersey City streets, jumping curbs and careening through vacant lots until he captured him. The police were called and the thief, whose pockets held twenty-five cents, a pack of cards and a pair of dice, was arrested.

Oscar Schmidt:
Musical Instrument Maker

My penchant for "old things" has found me trolling through rows of tables at outdoor flea markets on many an early morning hoping to discover antique treasures. Over the years, scanning those tables searching for something wonderful and scoring it at a bargain price meant a lot of talking with sellers and dealers. Those conversations, whether or not they led to a deal being struck and a purchase being made, were a real opportunity to learn from people who had amassed a great deal of information and expertise about the things they specialized in buying, collecting, and selling. That casually-acquired knowledge can come in handy . . . as it did when I was writing this story. How else would I have known what a "zither" is?

A zither is a stringed instrument dating to before the birth of Christ. Sometimes mistakenly referred to as an autoharp (a similar but distinct instrument), a zither may be played laid on a flat surface or propped in the player's lap and may have as few as a dozen strings or as many as 50, depending on the specific type. Zithers enjoyed a wave of popularity in the late 1800s and early 1900s and were found in many homes where they were used for parlor entertainment. A premier maker of zithers at that time was Oscar Schmidt, a German-born immigrant who formed a music publishing company in New Jersey in about 1879.

Schmidt, an astute businessman and entrepreneur, expanded his music publishing firm, opening a chain of music schools and using those schools to promote sheet music sales. He soon realized that he could then leverage his music school business by supplying instruments to the students. By the late 1890s, Schmidt was manufacturing zithers, mandolins, banjos and guitars at a large 30,000 square foot factory he opened on Ferry Street in Jersey City.

> WANTED—Girls 16 years of age, for light factory work. OSCAR SCHMIDT. 87-101 Ferry St., Jersey City.

In the early years of the 20th century, the Oscar Schmidt Company was among the largest manufacturers of stringed instruments with over a million instruments reportedly produced at the Jersey City factory and instrument sales around the world.

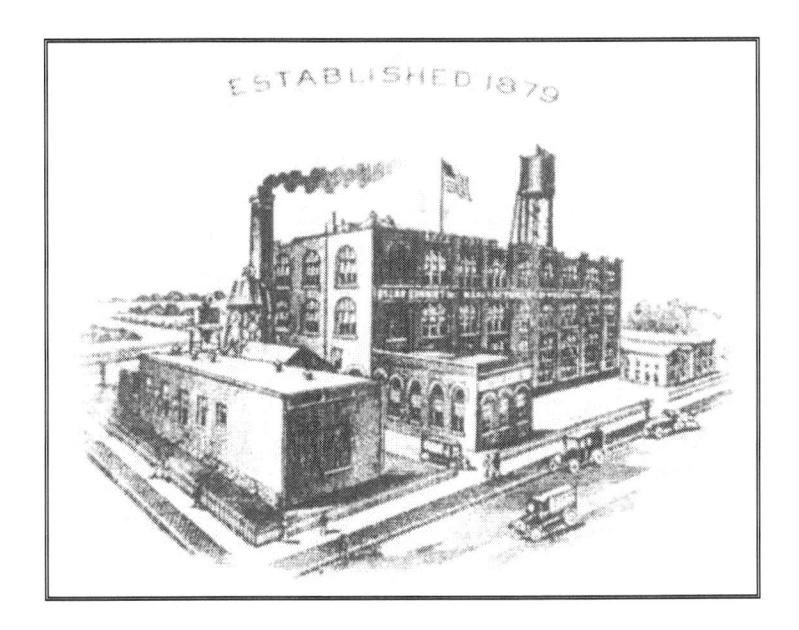

Schmidt Factory Jersey City

In addition to his success in the music business, Schmidt was an active investor in real estate. Among his property purchases, in 1900, was a large parcel and house on Palisade Avenue in what was then known as Hudson City. Extensive renovations were commenced by Schmidt, including raising a third story on the existing house, adding multiple bay windows, extending the dining room, and installing the latest in modern conveniences, including steam heat, electric lights, "ornamental fixtures and first-class bathrooms." The property was to have terraced landscaping with trees, flower beds and gravel walks and driveways. The cost of the work was expected to be at least $12-14,000.

There is no doubt that Oscar Schmidt, his wife and children were living very well as the result of Schmidt's hard work and business acumen but newspapers of the day did occasionally capture them dealing with life's ups and downs. In 1905, Mrs. Schmidt, accompanied by her daughter, drove out in their horse carriage with Mrs. Schmidt at the reins. Crossing Booream Avenue, the carriage was hit by a trolley. Mrs. Schmidt, who maintained that the motorman had not given any warning of the approaching trolley, somehow kept her head and control of the careening, damaged horse carriage, subduing the terrified horse and bringing the carriage to a stop. Cut and bruised, she was credited for her "skill and presence of mind" that prevented a much worse calamity.

Two years later, the Schmidts were involved in another vehicle-related incident when a horse and wagon belonging to Oscar went missing after being driven from Jersey City to New York by an employee, Louis Droove, who had taken a boy "helper" with him. When neither Droove or the boy – or the company horse and wagon – returned by the late evening, the police were notified. The following morning, the boy reappeared, telling the police that at 2am the previous night Droove had dropped him off on Barclay Street in New York saying that he should "beat it for the ferry and run home." The boy was unable to explain where they had been all day and night except to say that frequent stops were made at saloons. Some hours later, Jersey City Police were contacted by the 57th Precinct in Brooklyn saying they had found a "driverless horse and wagon bearing the name of Oscar Schmidt of Jersey City Heights." Droove, however, remained among the missing.

Oscar Schmidt died in 1929 while visiting one of his overseas factories, a month before the stock market crash and onset of the Great Depression, those events severely weakening the company which ultimately did not survive. Nonetheless, the Schmidt name and branding has lived on under the ownership of other instrument manufacturers to this day.

Oscar Schmidt came to New Jersey to pursue liberty and opportunities. Like so many immigrants before and after him, he brought his native culture and enterprising spirit to his new home, contributing to the diverse story of our state and America.

New Jersey Photographers:
Alfred Stieglitz & Theodore Gubelman

Returning from a trip to Italy a few years ago, I was surprised to discover that I had taken over 500 photographs while traveling. In these days of digital cameras, when concerns about the cost of film and developing are things of the past and memory cards hold hundreds of photos, we can snap away to our heart's content. This is a far cry from the early days of cameras in the 19th century when pioneer studio photographers ducked under a heavy black cloth in preparation for capturing the image of a carefully-posed subject.

Perhaps the most famous and celebrated American photographer of the late 19th and early 20th centuries was Alfred Stieglitz, born in Hoboken in 1864 to German immigrant parents. The 1870 U.S. census recorded the prosperous Stieglitz family, listed as having real estate valued at $6,000 and personal property valued at $2,000, residing in Hoboken's First Ward. In 1881 the family moved back to Europe where Alfred would abandon engineering school to pursue a newly-found fascination with photography, a decision that would lead to a remarkable 40-year career and photographic legacy second to none.

Alfred Stieglitz

Stieglitz is remembered not only as a master photographer with a body of work that captured images made dimensional by his own artistic expression, but also for his significant role as a promoter of the emerging modern art and artists of the early 20th century. Although his time as a resident of Hoboken ended early in his life, he was quoted in 1921 saying: "I was born in Hoboken. I am an American. Photography is my passion. The search for truth is my obsession."

While Stieglitz is the most famous early photographer from Hudson County, he was not the only notable one of the 19th century. Twenty years before Stieglitz was born, Theodore Gubelman was born on the German-Swiss border. A decade later, Gubelman and his parents emigrated to America and, when the 1860 U.S. census was taken, the family was living in Jersey City's Fourth Ward. Theodore, about 18, was employed as a lithographer and his father Joseph as a coppersmith. Not long after that census was taken, Theodore enlisted in the Union Army for a three-month tour and afterward briefly took a job in Tennessee taking photos of soldiers and other subjects. In 1864, the instability of conditions in the South sent him home to Jersey City where he opened his own photography studio and married. In the 1870s, a successful local photographer, Gubelman began exhibiting his work at photography fairs and his photos occasionally appeared in publications such as *Frank Leslie's Illustrated Newspaper*.

In 1874, local newspapers reported that he had been awarded a medal by the American Institute of Photography for an exhibit of his "fine imperial photographs" and, in August 1878, *The New York Times* reported that Gubelman had won a bronze medal at the Paris Exposition. Ironically, according to another newspaper report in January 1880, Gubelman had only then received that medal, some 17 months after winning it.

Gubelman Photo of the Brooklyn Bridge

Gubelman's 1890s studio, located at 77-79 Monmouth Street, and described as "one of the finest in the world" by the local press, reportedly included a winding staircase, "artistically appointed reception room," cherry woodwork, carpet into which "feet sank without a sound," and an "operating room with great glass skylights" with adjoining private toilette rooms for the ladies.

THEO. GUBELMAN,
PHOTOGRAPHER,
41 Newark Avenue.
FIRST DOOR ABOVE THE CITY HALL, JERSEY CITY.
Photographs in all sizes, plain or coloured, in oil or water. Cartes de Visite, Ambrotypes, Ivory types.
PORCELAIN PICTURES.
Particular attention paid to copying and taking Children's Pictures.
A Full Stock of
FRAMES AND CASES.

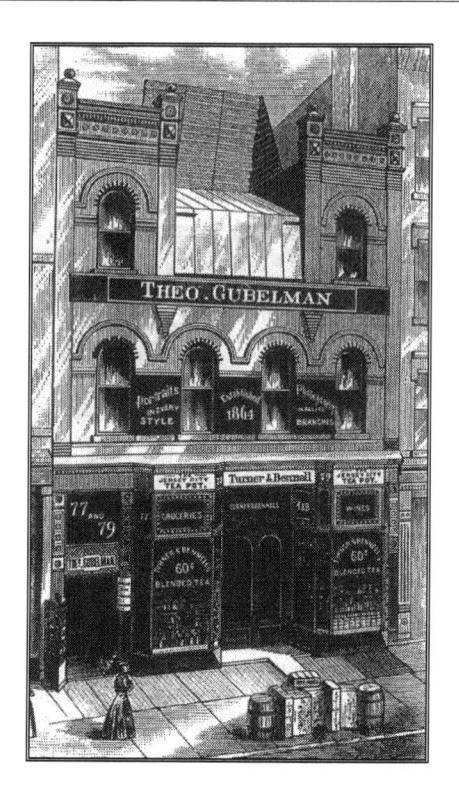

Gubelman was not the only local studio photographer however. Others of the period from the 1860s on included the Insley Gallery, also on Monmouth Street, A.C. Lewis and A.B. Costello on Newark Avenue, Victor Piard on Grand Street and E.B. Monckton in the Heights. Examples of their pocket-size studio portraits survive, giving us a different manner of "snapshot" of locals of more than a century ago, dressed in their best but usually unsmiling. Perhaps the photographers, absorbed with their new-fangled and complex equipment neglected to say "cheese" before capturing their subjects for posterity.

In 1901, Gubelman unexpectedly found himself a player in a sensational criminal court case arising from a complaint against the Bon Ton Theatre for the display of "immorally suggestive" posters advertising a burlesque revue entitled "Satan's Inn." He was one of about 15 citizens, including clergy, a female school principal, library president, merchants, lawyers and an Assemblyman, requested to come to the court to view the offensive posters and give an opinion as to their artistic "character." Also on the committee was the poster artist himself, one Henry Harrison, a professional artist whose work brings respectable prices even today. Brouhaha notwithstanding, some weeks later, the Grand Jury declined to indict and the Bon Ton was exonerated, no doubt grateful for the free publicity generated by the episode.

Simon "King" Kelly: Weehawken Political Force

I am a lover of books as well as writing. Among my favorite authors is Frank Delaney, the prize-winning, best-selling author who NPR dubbed "The Most Eloquent Man in the World." Said more succinctly, Delaney, in the tradition of his Irish roots, can really tell a story. In his book *Venetia Kelly's Traveling Show*, he weaves a 1930s tale of a mesmerizing woman and her immoral, parasitic family. One of the key characters is "King" Kelly, a smooth-as-glass con-man and sometime politician whose greed and propensity for using people make him as dangerous as the most venomous snake. Never expecting it, I recently came across another "King" Kelly who was a politician, this one a real person who twice served as the Mayor of Weehawken in the late 19th century.

Simon "King" Kelly was born in Ireland in 1848 during the worst years of the Great Irish Famine which likely explains why he emigrated to America with his parents within a year after his birth. The Kelly family was living in Hoboken at the time of the 1850 U.S. census and Simon's father was listed as a blacksmith. A few years later, the Kellys moved to Weehawken where Simon would live the rest of his life.

In December 1871, Simon Kelly married his wife Ann at St. Michael's R.C. Church in Union City. At the time of the 1880 U.S. census, Simon and Ann and their young children were living on Old Dock Row in Weehawken.

Simon "King" Kelly

Simon Kelly was reportedly active in Weehawken politics beginning as soon as he was first eligible to vote and was a staunch life-long Democrat. At age 22, he held his first elective office, Poormaster, and served in that capacity for three years. Over the ensuing 25 years, he would serve on the Township Committee, as a School

Trustee, Fire Chief and Police Chief, as Mayor of Weehawken twice (1885-1889 and 1891-1897) and as a Freeholder in the 1890s. No wonder he was dubbed the King of Weehawken!

In 1895, a local newspaper carried an article titled "Saint Simon Kelly" with the subtitle "He Made Hundreds of Children at Snake Hill Happy." Freeholder Kelly had made a practice of visiting the Almshouse at Snake Hill at Christmas, dressing up as Santa Claus. In support of his disguise, he donned 24-inch stilts making himself quite literally an imposing, larger-than-life Kris Kringle. As he arrived armed with large bags of toys, the children of the Almshouse ran to greet him. Assisted by another Freeholder, Kelly gave each grateful child a toy and a bag filled with candy, nuts and oranges.

Kelly was known for his charity and there were many stories of his kindnesses to his constituents and some talk that it came at the expense of his own financial condition. He only lost one election in his 25-year political career, that happening at the end of his long years of service to the people of Weehawken. He then retired and focused his time and efforts on operating the local hotel he had built several years earlier, Kelly's Point View Hotel at Clifton Park.

Simon Kelly, age 52 and seemingly in good health, fell ill with peritonitis in late May 1900 and died within days thereafter at the Point View Hotel where he lived. A headline in a local newspaper announced the death of the "King of Weehawken" recalling his nearly three-decade political career and generosity and kindness to the poor and distressed. Just months after Kelly's death, the Clifton and Highwood Hose Companies responded to a midnight fire at the Point View and were successful in saving the hotel from destruction as a crowd of prominent Weehawken citizens and officials looked on.

Kelly's Point View Hotel

Hudson County Theatres & Movie Houses

My mother Arlene was a "Jersey Girl" decades before anyone thought of calling us Garden State girls by the moniker that now evokes images of big hair and dark suntans. Arlene wasn't that kind of "Jersey Girl." She was a Jersey *City* girl, born and raised. Born just weeks after the stock market crash of 1929, a child of the Depression and an adolescent of World War II, my mother remembers a very happy, if modest, childhood in the city she loved, surrounded by caring family, friends and neighbors in the Greenville section. I enjoy hearing her talk about those "old days" and I am usually the one to prompt her to tell me those stories.

Arlene is now a girl of 84. Not long ago we were having lunch and as she neatly constructed a petite sandwich for herself, I asked her to tell me what she did for fun when she was a teenager in the mid/late 1940s. She looked up and thought for a moment. "Well, we went to dances at the 'Y' and other places, went to the movies and always stopped in to hang out at 'our' soda fountain." She explained that there were soda fountains all over Jersey City and that young people had their favorites where they knew they would meet up with friends.

"Where did you go to the movies?" I asked, knowing that Jersey City has a rich history of early movie theatres. After reminding me that her memory isn't as good as it once was, she told me about going to the Cameo on Ocean Avenue, near Cator Avenue. I don't remember the Cameo, although we lived in Greenville until I was five years old. I do remember coming back to Jersey City to stay with my maternal grandparents during summer vacations and taking the bus to Journal Square with my grandmother to see a movie at the wonderful Stanley theatre.

Curiosity piqued, I dug around a bit to find out more about those iconic houses of live shows and cinema that entertained people for many years before falling victim to perceived obsolescence by the 1960s and 70s. Most of the best remembered theatres, including the Stanley, Loew's, State, Palace, Capitol and Cameo, opened during the Roaring Twenties and began their runs showcasing live acts in the days of Vaudeville and early movies. The largest and most lavish were architectural and interior design works of art, and no doubt prompted many wide eyes and dropping jaws among theatre-goers, even before the curtain came up.

Two decades before these grand movie houses opened their doors, however, there was already a lively theatre community in Jersey City, Bayonne, and Hoboken that included the Majestic Theatre, Bon Ton Theatre and Academy of Music, all in Jersey City, the Gayety Theatre and Empire in Hoboken and the Bayonne Opera House. The Majestic, located at Grove and Montgomery Streets, opened in September 1907 to raves.

Months before that, the *Jersey Journal* reported "Curious Crowds at Majestic Theatre," gathering daily to watch the progress of construction at the new playhouse building that would seat over 2,000 people and include dressing rooms to accommodate 200. The "curious" included not only locals but "architects in charge of new playhouses in other cities." The *Journal* went on to describe construction specifics that would result in a brick and masonry building "far in excess of the requirements of new building laws."

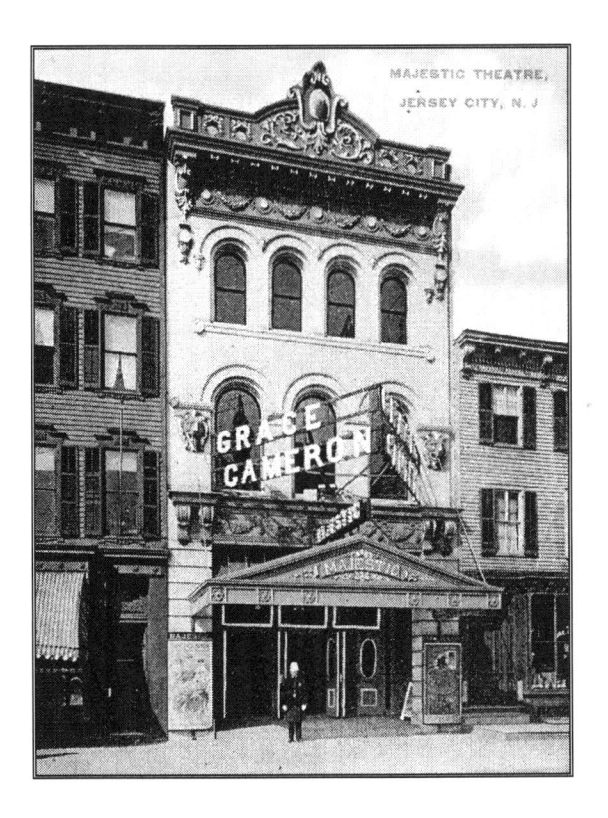

The *Journal* also covered opening night at the Majestic under the headline "A Brilliant Audience at the Majestic," reporting that "the consensus of opinion was that the latest addition to Jersey City's dramatic temples was a credit to all concerned." A hundred years ago, locals could have gone to the Majestic to see Fiske O'Hara, "America's favorite Irish singing comedian," in the romantic comedy-drama "The Wearing of the Green", to the Bon Ton for "Bohemian Burlesque" or to the Bayonne Opera House where "Uncle Tom's Cabin" was finishing its run. The Empire Theatre was offering vaudeville, "nifty girls," and "sensational acrobats."

```
BON TON THEATRE
T.W. DINKINS — JERSEY CITY, N.J. — MANAGER
WHERE THE PEOPLE GO
NEXT ATTRACTION
MONDAY, TUESDAY AND WEDNESDAY, SEPT. 5, 6 & 7. MAT. EVERY DAY
THE TIGER LILIES CO.
WITH
MATT KENNEDY
"Everybody's Favorite."
ADDED ATTRACTION
ZALLAH
"The Dancing Venus."
THURSDAY, FRIDAY AND SATURDAY, SEPT. 8, 9 & 10. MAT. EVERY DAY
TOM MINER'S
BOHEMIAN BURLESQUERS
WITH ANDY GARDNER (Our Old Friend Patsy) and IDA NICOLA (as Rosie) in
THE BELLE OF THE BOARDING SCHOOL
—AND—
PATSY IN PARIS
OUR ALL-STAR OLIO—Valnors sisters, Bernard and Dunham, Lawrence and Thompson, Bohemian Quartet.
EXTRA ADDED FEATURE—AH-LING-FOO—THE WONDER WORKER.
NIGHT PRICES—15c to 75c
Special Bargain Matinees—All Seats 25c
```

Then, as now, a play, movie, or musical entertainment could (temporarily) transport its audience out of their own lives, daily cares and struggles through the talent and creativity of writers, musicians, and performers. Given the choice, I wonder if they would have traded their seats at the Majestic for the chance to watch "Dancing with the Stars" on an Ipad.

The Titanic Disaster

Some fifteen years ago, I was among the wave of millions who flocked to theaters to see James Cameron's epic film, *Titanic,* an unqualified hit that brought the story of the 1912 tragedy back to life. April 15, 2012 marked 100 years since the tragic deaths of 1,500 passengers and crew who lost their lives in the dark, biting-cold waters of the Atlantic, and that anniversary rekindled widespread interest in the story once again. Part of the lure of this true story is its magnitude and scale: an "unsinkable" ship on its maiden voyage, thousands of passengers, among them the rich and famous and those scraping by in steerage class hoping for a new start in America. No work of fiction launched from the creative recesses of a novelist's mind or a screenwriter's imagination could better convey the seeming randomness and unpredictability of life and death.

Among the Titanic passengers were a number of New Jersey residents including a Union Hill governess and young Bayonne bartender who both survived and a 21-year-old man from Hoboken and a 23-year-old man from Jersey City who did not. Each of the young men who had lost his life had booked passage on the Titanic after visiting his mother, one in London and the other in County Longford, Ireland. The loss to be endured by the Irish mother, Mrs. Kiernan, was cruelly multiplied by the fact that a second son, hearing his expatriate brother's glowing descriptions of life in America, decided to accompany him back to the States and also lost his life when the Titanic went down.

The young bartender from Bayonne, Thomas McCormack, was also returning from a trip to his Irish homeland. Unlike his neighbors from Hoboken and Jersey City, Thomas had the good fortune of being plucked from the icy waters of the Atlantic Ocean by the crew of the ship Carpathia and lived to be reunited with three sisters living on West Twentieth Street in Bayonne.

Miss Elizabeth Dowdell, of Park Ave in Union Hill (now Union City), a 31-year-old governess, boarded the Titanic in Southampton England, traveling in a third class cabin along with her charge, 6-

year-old Virginia, the daughter of opera singer Estelle Emmanuel. Both escaped the sinking ship after being carried bodily aboard lifeboat number 13 and subsequently being rescued by the Carpathia. Arriving in New York, the governess wept as she delivered Virginia into the arms of the child's grateful grandparents. Elizabeth then returned home to the elation of her own mother in Union Hill and was interviewed by reporters from several local newspapers. Her chilling, first-person account of the massive liner's final death throes sheds light on the terror gripping the seventy desperate souls wedged into lifeboat 13 in the cold and darkness:

"I had put Virginia to bed and was preparing to retire when the crash came . . . a terrible shiver went through the ship. I went to the passageway and asked a steward what was wrong. He assured me everything was all right and scarcely had I closed the door before someone came running along the passage ordering all hands to dress and put on a life belt. I took time getting ready. I firmly believed Titanic was unsinkable.

When we tried to get to the deck, the stairways were so crowded that we could not use them . . . the cries and curses were terrible to hear. Finally some of the men passengers realized it would be impossible to get up the stairways and hoisted women and children up to seamen on the gallery above. When we arrived on deck nearly all of the boats were off but we were carried onto number 13. Several men tried to rush in on us before we were lowered. I saw an officer shoot three of them.

We plainly saw the iceberg and the gaping hole in the side of the ship . . . the sea rushed in in torrents. No sooner were we off than the Titanic began to go down rapidly, the bow disappearing first. There was no playing by the bands . . . only the cries and sobs of those still aboard and in the boats heard above the wash of the sea."

Elizabeth Dowdell lived a long life and in December 1958, at age 78, attended the New York premiere of the movie "A Night to Remember," the first feature film about the Titanic disaster.

Rosie the Riveter:

NJ Women in the War Effort

In my historical and genealogical research, I often encounter old photos that draw me in or pique my curiosity and send me reaching for a magnifying glass to get a closer look at faces, clothing and background detail. They say "a picture is worth a thousand words." In the case of this column, about 700 words were inspired by an old circa 1918 photo of four Jersey girls working at a local railroad yard.

Most of us are familiar with Rosie the Riveter, a fictional female cultural icon representing the persona of millions of American women who responded to the call to take on non-traditional jobs during World War II. In 1942, a popular song written by Evans and Loeb and titled "Rosie the Riveter" first gave life to Rosie and included the lyrics *"All the day long, whether rain or shine, she's part of the assembly line. She's making history, working for victory, Rosie the Riveter."* In May, 1943, Norman Rockwell gave Rosie a face on the cover of the *Saturday Evening Post* although the image of Rosie that remains the most well-known and recognized is the one featured on a U.S. government war poster with the slogan "We Can Do It."

The need being so pressing, a broad spectrum of women responded to the call to work: single, married, with and without children and even those newly-graduated from high school. Women already in the workforce in lower paying traditionally female jobs often switched to higher paying factory jobs in response to the need to fill those ranks. Their contributions to the war effort were essential, invaluable and never to be forgotten.

As it turns out, the "Rosies" of World War II were second-generation home-front heroines, following in the footsteps of women who stepped up to the very same challenge during World War I. During that earlier war, women were actively recruited to work for the railroads, including large carriers like the Pennsylvania Railroad and Baltimore & Ohio and smaller local lines, filling in for men gone into the military.

A World War I era photo capturing the smiling faces of four young women "car cleaners" in overalls and caps posing in the window of a train car at the Jersey City railroad yard had brought an immediate involuntary smile to my face. It also sent me on a trip through newspaper archives to read more about these rail ladies where I learned that they, like their later counterparts in World War II, were sorely needed to take on key non-traditional jobs in the absence of the men who vacated them. I also found that, during both wars, while there was no dispute as to the absolute need for women to step in to fill jobs, there was a natural tension that led to newspaper articles and editorials pointing out that the women were only to be in these jobs temporarily and must relinquish them to the men returning from wartime service.

So what did these World War I rail ladies do? The *Philadelphia Inquirer* ran a piece in July, 1917 about the upset resulting from the hiring of "young and middle-aged, pretty and passable" women as ticket sellers, crossing guards, gate tenders, car cleaners, car-shop workers, signal operators, flagmen and freight office clerks for the West Jersey & Seashore Railroad. According to the article, commuters missed their trains, forgot tickets at the ticket window and just plain got flustered at the sight of the women rail workers. It went on to say that customers might get a "whiff of talcum powder instead of tobacco" with the addition of female workers and predicted, tongue in cheek, that lace curtains and window boxes at watchman crossing shelters might come later. The *Inquirer* did interview some of the rail ladies including Virginia Miller, a New Jersey ticket seller, who said, reportedly with a toss of her head, that the "girls" were going to show that they could "hold down their jobs just as well as the men." As Miss Miller was speaking her mind, a male customer came to her window, requested a ticket and, upon taking it and looking up to see Virginia, promptly walked away without his change. She "coolly called him back" and gave it to him.

You go girl!

The Featherstone Gang

In the bad old days of the mid-1800s, New York City had its infamous gangs like those depicted in the memorable film, *Gangs of New York*. Its neighbor across the Hudson was no different. In the 19th century, Jersey City was home to many gangs who claimed specific streets and neighborhoods as their turf. These hoodlums instilled fear in residents and business owners, committing robbery, burglary, assault, extortion and even murder. Those they victimized were afraid to testify against them, making it difficult for law enforcement to arrest and incarcerate them. One of the worst of these Jersey City gangs was the Lava Beds, also known as the Featherstone gang, that operated in what was then the Sixth Ward, a poor immigrant neighborhood.

The Featherstone boys were the sons of Michael and Catherine Ivers Featherstone, born in Ireland in the 1830s. Survivors of the Irish Famine, they arrived in New Jersey in the 1860s and were parents to six sons and a daughter. The family lived in rented rooms in Jersey City in the 400-block of First Street.

The seven Featherstone children cut their teeth in that tough Sixth Ward neighborhood and nothing good came from the lessons they learned there. The older Featherstone boys were petty thieves before the age of ten and soon graduated to robbery and larceny. In their mid-teens, the four oldest boys became the heart of the Lava Beds gang.

In 1880, when the census-taker made his way down First Street interviewing each family, most of them, including the Featherstone family of nine, were headed by Irish immigrants. Michael Featherstone Sr. was listed as a laborer and his wife as "keeping house." Sons James, 18, and Michael Jr., 16, were listed as "in Reform School" at Jamesburg.

James Featherstone

The Lava Beds and other gangs in Jersey City created a pervasive climate of fear in poor neighborhoods. Mothers were afraid to let their children play outside for fear of violence or their young boys being recruited by gang members. Women were accosted on the street and became victim to lewd remarks and even sexual overtures and assaults by these brazen gang members, making it unsafe to go out alone even in the daytime hours. The Lava Beds, like so many criminal gangs before and after them, operated in their own backyard . . . literally . . . preying on and brutalizing their "own kind," ethnically and economically. Utterly without a moral compass or conscience, they passed the time and amused themselves by stealing socks one minute and beating a pregnant woman nearly to death the next.

Police raids, repetitive arrests and incarcerations notwithstanding, the Featherstone boys rode the revolving door of justice like a carousel, moving in and out of the judicial and prison systems time and time again. They no sooner were released than were back at it again – thieving, breaking and entering, assaulting, vandalizing, extorting businesses and the like. The *New York Herald* followed the escapades of the Lava Beds and the Featherstones, describing them as the "most persistent and notorious gang of law breakers that the Jersey City police have to deal with" and saying that although half the gang was then in State Prison for crimes including highway robbery and burglary, "they manage, however, to recruit for their ranks and fill the places made vacant by the retirement of the veterans to prison." By the late 1880s, the Featherstones had been terrorizing the Sixth Ward for the better part of a decade and reportedly had no "home," just drifting around the neighborhood, living as squatters in vacant apartments.

In the succeeding decade from 1889 on, the headlines kept coming, even as the four oldest Featherstones passed through their twenties, thirties and early forties. Assault, battery, burglary, larceny, robbery and all manner of mayhem were recounted in newspapers of the day. After that, the trail goes cold and I found no trace of the Featherstone "boys" in local census or other public records. Persistent, pernicious predators, they may have fled the area to avoid arrest or ended up as non-descript dead in the streets and alleys they haunted, falling victim to the excesses of their wasted lives.

19th Century New Jersey Yacht Clubs

It's summer in Jersey. How do I know? First, I have over 30 heirloom tomato plants sprouting yellow blossoms in my backyard garden and even though it will be weeks before they turn into the tastiest tomatoes anywhere, I have visions of BLTs dancing in my head. Second, I now time my visits to my mother in Ocean County with the specific objective of avoiding the sea of people on the Parkway heading down to the Shore to cultivate a tan, cruise the boardwalk, or enjoy swimming and boating.

The draw of our state's coastal waters as a venue for family outings, water sports or the opportunity to step aboard and spend a day fishing or lounging on deck has been a long-standing constant of life in New Jersey, north and south. New Jersey, for instance, was home to many yacht clubs in the 19th century, some of those organized just before and after the Civil War.

The Oceanic Yacht Club was formed in 1871 and had its club house at the foot of Henderson Street in Jersey City. In 1878, its fleet included 13 sailing yachts, one catamaran, and one steam launch and the club numbered about 40 members. Still active 20 years later, in 1899 the club had over 60 members, a fleet of 18 vessels, and had purchased a site at the foot of Communipaw Avenue on which an attractive new club house was to be built.

The Hudson Yacht Club was organized in 1877, its original incorporators almost entirely made up of county and city officials including Sheriff P. H. Laverty and Judge Hoffman. That same year the Club purchased, at a cost of $4,000, a steam yacht measuring 51 feet long and 10.5 feet wide, naming the vessel Annie L. after the Sheriff's wife. A steam yacht was chosen to avoid the nuisance of dealing with poor wind conditions and the Annie L. served the club members well, carrying them on excursions to seaside resorts, her larder stocked with food and a good selection of wines to insure a pleasant journey. Roughing it this was not.

PAVONIA YACHT CLUB, BAYONNE, N. J.

Regattas were sponsored by the various yacht clubs as pleasure outings or competitions. In 1870, the Bayonne Yacht Club held its 4th annual regatta, hosting 15 yachts from its own membership along with others affiliated with the Oceanic, Brooklyn, Americus, Atlantic, Union and Harlem Yacht Clubs. Two decades later in May

1896, multiple regattas marked the opening of the boating season. The Pavonia Yacht Club regatta set off from Jersey City racing to Sandy Hook for a celebration there. The Oceanic Yacht Club held its regatta on a 10-mile course mapped out on the waters of Newark Bay. The Jersey City Yacht Club observed their long-time tradition of a short sail followed by a chowder dinner.

Currier & Ives – Regatta

There is one more yacht club I should mention, as I believe it may have a personal connection to my family: the Newark Bay Yacht Club. In 1909, that club held a reception celebrating the opening of its new club house located on Pearsall Avenue at Newark Bay in the Greenville section of Jersey City. Nearly a half-century later when I was born at the Margaret Hague, my parents brought me home to a very modest, flat-top, red-shingled home located at the foot of

Pearsall Avenue next to the railroad tracks and Newark Bay, a building that had started life as a club house.

The "Red House" with Roosevelt Stadium in the background

The "Red House" as we all called it, was leased to my grandparents by the railroad for one dollar a year. My mother and her five brothers spent most of their happy childhood in the Red House during and after the Depression and my mother's wedding photos capture her coming down its no-frills porch steps. In the 1950s, my father, barbecuing too close to those red shingles, set the place on fire. When my mother tells the fire story, she always mentions that I had been napping inside just before the shingles went up and, but for her having picked me up from my crib and taken me out into the yard with her, I might have been toast. Jersey City's brave firemen saved the Red House from destruction although the water and smoke damage made for quite a clean-up.

I cannot say for certain that three generations of my Jersey City family lived many happy days at what was once the Newark Bay Yacht Club but, if you checked the 1940 census records, you would see that my grandparents lived in the last house at the foot of Pearsall Avenue, next to Newark Bay.

New Jersey Irish-American Boxers: Cal McCarthy & Frankie Burns

While researching my second book, *Young & Wicked*, I spent many hours ferreting out and reading 19th century newspaper stories related to one of the central characters, Willie Flannelly, Jersey City bad boy and my great-grandmother's second cousin. Among the various true stories of his juvenile delinquency and anti-social behavior was one recounting him using a slungshot blow to the head to knock out a popular local featherweight boxer named Cal McCarthy. Different from a *slingshot*, a slungshot was a maritime tool consisting of a weight attached to a heavy cord that later became a favorite concealed weapon of thugs in the late 1800s. Ah, the misguided ingenuity of the criminal mind.

Callahan J. McCarthy was born in Pennsylvania in 1867 and came to the Horseshoe section of Jersey City with his Irish immigrant parents about five years later. One of six children, he made his first public appearance as an amateur boxer in 1887 in association with the Scottish-American Club of Jersey City. A bare knuckles fighter and all of 5' 2" and 100 pounds, he won the American amateur 110-pound championship that year and turned pro in early 1888.

McCarthy, called the "Wonder," had a great left jab and quick cat-like movements. He went on to fight more than 40 bouts in various venues around the country, taking on both American and European opponents and won the Featherweight Championship of America.

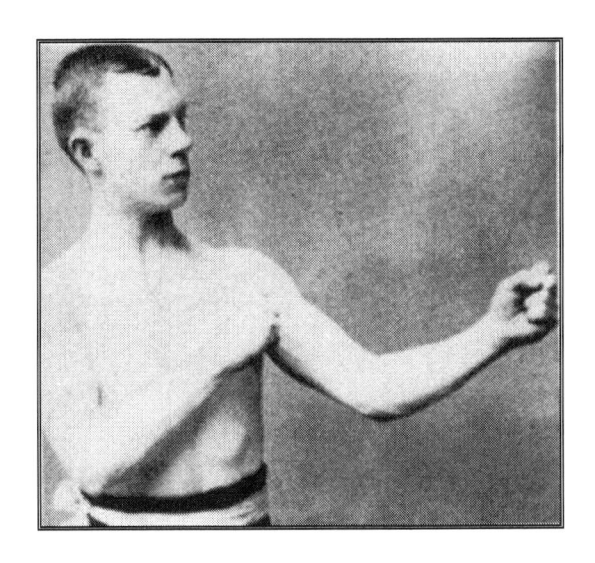

Cal McCarthy

In 1890 in Boston, he took on George Dixon in a bout that went on for 70 rounds until a draw was declared. In their second meeting in 1891, Dixon beat McCarthy in 22 rounds. Following that defeat, McCarthy reportedly turned to drinking, soon losing his form and discipline but still fighting sporadically. The young boxer never regained his stride, was stricken with tuberculosis and, still planning a boxing comeback, died in 1895 at 28 years old. Despite that, he was remembered by fight fans and sports writers who, two decades later, still reminisced about McCarthy when talking about the latest crop of young featherweight and bantam boxers.

In 1889, as McCarthy was turning pro, another Irish-American boy and future pugilist, Francis (Frankie) Burns was born in Jersey City. By 1910, the Burns family, living on First Street according to the 1910 U.S. census, was headed by 20-year-old Frankie Burns, a "helper" at an express company, and included his twice-widowed mother Mary and several younger siblings.

Burns had started boxing in 1908 and in January 1911, at 5'5" and weighing in at 117 pounds, Burns fought Englishman Digger Stanley, the British bantam champion, in a ten-round bout at New York's National Sporting Club. Newspapers covering the Burns-Stanley match mentioned Burns' rise from "tail boy" working the back end of Adams Express wagons to world champion contender in less than a year, describing the fight as "one of the greatest boxing bouts ever seen in this country between two little men," and reporting that when the bell rang for the last round, "the crowd was on its feet" and "cheers almost shook the building." While local papers called Burns the "practical winner" of the fight, boxing records call it a "no decision" or draw.

A week after the Stanley fight, the *Wilkes-Barre* (Pennsylvania) *Times* carried a piece titled "Frankie Burns – Great Bantam – Bread Winner of Family." The article described Burns as a "clean living and ambitious young fellow" who had come from obscurity to within sight of a championship in just three years despite losing his father at age 5 and working since he was 11 to help support his mother and siblings, including paying medical bills for a handicapped sister.

Known as a talented, quick and clever boxer, Burns fought as both a bantam and featherweight and, in over a decade in the ring, had more than 150 matches as a consistent championship contender, taking on other top boxers of the day including Johnny Coulon, Eddie Campi and Johnny Kilbane.

BOXING

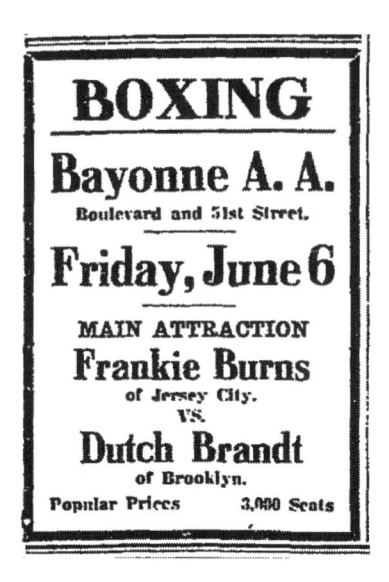

Bayonne A. A.
Boulevard and 51st Street.

Friday, June 6

MAIN ATTRACTION

Frankie Burns
of Jersey City.
vs.
Dutch Brandt
of Brooklyn.

Popular Prices   3,000 Seats

Burns was often compared to Cal McCarthy, one newspaper describing Burns as "the greatest little fighting man New Jersey has produced since Cal McCarthy, the idol of the Horseshoe." The well-respected fighter passed away in 1961 at age 71 and, in 1969, he was inducted into the New Jersey Boxing Hall of Fame.

Isaac Edge:

1812 Drummer Boy & Pyrotechnist

The War of 1812, sometimes referred to as the second American war for independence, typically gets little attention and, for the general public, doesn't evoke the images or specifics that come to mind when the Civil War or Revolutionary War is mentioned. The next 700 or so words will recall the War of 1812 to mind as I share the story of a New Jersey veteran of that war, a windmill, and the family pyrotechnics enterprise.

The War of 1812 began with a declaration of war from the young United States government in response to Britain's interference with our trade with France and its impressments of naturalized American sailors into British military service by force. Early in the conflict, U.S. forces attacked Canada, a British colony. In 1814, British forces invaded the U.S., capturing Washington and burning the Capitol and White House. American troops repulsed British attacks on New York, Baltimore and New Orleans and, in early 1815, the war ended with the Treaty of Ghent. New Jersey Militia units fought in the War of 1812, including Captain Samuel Smith's Infantry Company, part of the Third Regiment. Young Isaac Edge Jr., born in 1800 in England, served in Smith's unit as the company drummer boy.

Bergen County.		Captain Samuel M. Smith's Company of Infantry. Third Regiment New Jersey Detailed Militia.			
1	Samuel M. Smith	Captain	Sept. 19, '14	For the war	Dec. 2, '14
1	John F. Watkins	Lieut.	"	"	"
1	John Farr (or Fair)	Ensign	"	"	"
1	Uriah Jenkins	Sergeant	"	"	"
2	Halstead Lawrence	"	"	"	"
3	Henry Dakin	"	"	"	"
4	John Lovinss	"	"	"	"
1	David Hinman	Corporal	"	"	"
2	Samuel Cook	"	"	"	"
3	John Griffiths	"	"	"	"
4	Joshua B. Miller	"	"	"	"
1	John Pierre	Drummer	"	"	"
1	John Cook, Jr.	Fifer	"	"	"
1	Bisset, George	Private	"	"	"
2	Bryant, Gifford	"	"	"	"
3	Cassady, Quintillian	"	"	"	"
4	Crane, Daniel	"	"	"	"
5	Culley, John	"	"	"	"
6	Daniels, Bradley	"	"	"	"
7	Daniels, John	"	"	"	"
8	Durant, Samuel	"	"	"	"
9	Edge, Isaac	"	"	"	"
10	Egbert, Peter	"	"	"	"
11	Fogal, George	"	"	"	"

Isaac Edge Jr. was the namesake of his father, Isaac Sr., who immigrated from Derbyshire, England with his wife Frances and baby son in about 1801, settling in Paulus Hook by 1806. The elder Edge, a baker and miller by trade like his own father, built a large windmill on the corner of Montgomery and Green Streets in about 1815 and used it to produce high quality flour for locals and others who brought their grain for milling by ship.

The Edge Windmill

Edge Jr., the teenage drummer boy, did not follow his father and grandfather into the milling business and all indications are that he remained possessed of an independent and adventurous spirit. By the 1830s, he was the successful owner of a well-known pyrotechnics company located in Jersey City and was also a hobbyist hot air balloonist whose exploits were covered in newspapers of the day. In September 1837, Edge ascended in a balloon from Hoboken, reaching an altitude of 8,000 feet, drifting over New York City and landing on a farm in Flatbush.

Edge was also an inventor. In the late 1840s, he invented an "article of fire alarm," to be carried by police officers at night. Not the kind of fire alarm we would think of, this was carried in the pocket and could be taken out and struck against a hard surface to emit a bright light. He also developed a new form of portable rocket device that would propel a bomb a distance of up to two miles.

He was best known as an important "pyrotechnist." His Jersey City fireworks company was a premier provider of lavish fireworks displays in major U.S. cities including New York and Boston. The 4th of July fireworks program on Boston Common in 1846 was presented by Isaac Edge and his company. It closed with a fireworks depiction of the 16th century Castle of San Juan de Ulua (Veracruz, Mexico) measuring 100 feet in length and costing $2,000.

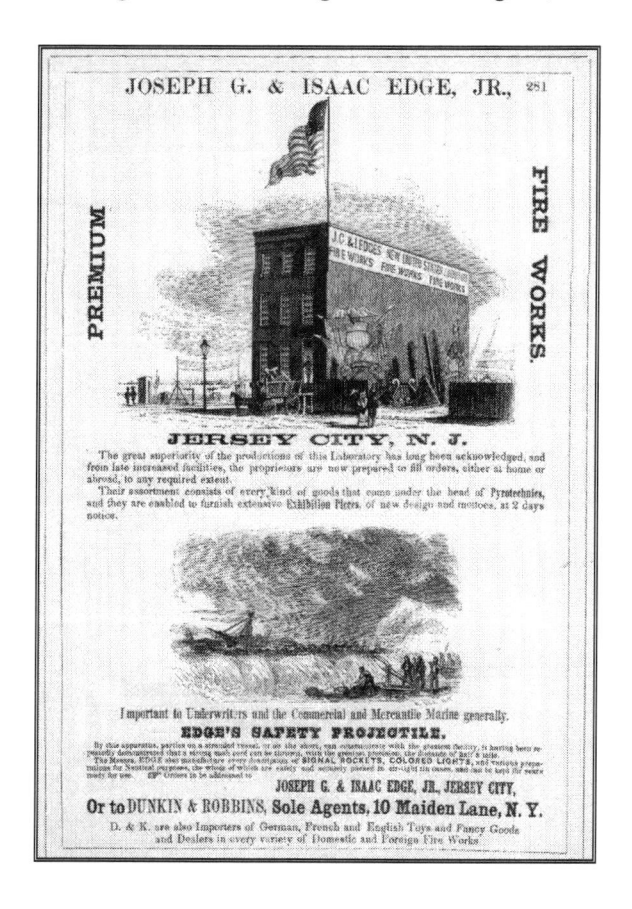

The descriptions of Edge's Boston fireworks program two years earlier were published in large newspaper advertisements. Included were no less than 40 separate displays with exotic names like *Egyptian Pyramids of Roman Candles, Night Blooming Ceres, Peruvian Cross, Vulcan's Frolic – Dance of Fire,* and *Chinese Pagoda*. The finale was titled *The Temple of Liberty*, described as being 200 feet long, the center standing 56 feet off the ground and including a 14-foot star bearing the inscription "Go Tell the World America is Free!" In total, the display was to cover over 60,000 square feet and finish with a "grand flight of 120 rockets, colored stars and gold rain."

Isaac Edge

Isaac Edge Jr. died at age 58 in March, 1859 in Jersey City and is interred at the Jersey City Harsimus Cemetery. His fireworks firm remained in business for many years under the management of his son. In 1917, nearly 60 years after Edge passed away, a local newspaper ran a story titled "Where Dad Got His Fireworks," recounting the Edge pyrotechnics story as originally reported in the *Jersey City Advertiser* in 1838.

Snake Hill:

An All-Too-Common Legacy

In the 1800s (and earlier), the concept of "political correctness" had yet to be born. Newspapers recounted the happenings of the day in a style that often blended fact, conjecture and editorial opinion as if all three were equal in contribution to the accurate telling of the story. Likewise the description of people's behavior (e.g. "painted ladies lounging in dives") and institutions (e.g. "lunatic asylum").

Speaking of "lunatic asylums," that brings us to the subject of this story: the Snake Hill complex once located in Secaucus, New Jersey. In my years of genealogical researching, I have found myself "visiting" Snake Hill multiple times. Anyone with New Jersey family roots may well have a Snake Hill connection in their own family. Snake Hill, located in Secaucus adjacent to what is now the New Jersey Turnpike, was a complex of penal and charitable institution buildings opened by Hudson County beginning in the 1850s, the last of them closed in 1962. The facilities consisted of a penitentiary with a quarry where prisoners were put to work, a "lunatic asylum" and an almshouse (poorhouse).

By the early 20th century during the days when "consumption" was rampant, it would also include a tuberculosis and contagious diseases hospital. For the many indigent inmates who did not survive their stay at one of the Snake Hill facilities, there was also a burial ground on the site. Hundreds of people lived at the Snake Hill facilities at any one time and many thousands did so over the century that these institutions were in operation. Snake Hill, later renamed (more pleasantly) Laurel Hill, was essentially a community of last resort for so many of its inmates, particularly in the 19th and early 20th centuries. Many of those inmates were non-English-speaking immigrants who must have been surprised and frightened as the massive complex first came into sight.

Think it's unlikely that your Jersey roots found their way to Snake Hill? Consider the following. In researching my Irish family line, I discovered that my great-grandfather Whalen's second wife died at the Snake Hill Tuberculosis Hospital in the early 1920s. My great-great-grandfather Flannelly's youngest brother died in the almshouse in about 1915. My great-grandmother Flannelly-Whalen's second cousin Margaret was an inmate of the Snake Hill Lunatic Asylum for about twenty years, dying there in 1927. Margaret's brother William was incarcerated at the Snake Hill Penitentiary in the late 1880s. The good news for those four Snake Hill "residents" was that each of them left Snake Hill (three dead, one alive) and did not end up interred there. For thousands of others, Snake Hill was their last stop……literally. They went through the doors of the asylum, medical hospitals, almshouse or prison and came out in a pine box, buried on the Snake Hill grounds. Nearly ten thousand people were buried at Snake Hill, including indigents who died on the streets of Jersey City, Hoboken and other Hudson County locales (think "Potter's Field").

While a charity burial is a humane thing, the dead of Snake Hill have not always been left to "rest in peace." Progress, in the form of the New Jersey Turnpike, has rolled over them……sometimes literally. The New Jersey Turnpike Authority, an empire unto itself and arguably one of New Jersey's most insular and mistrusted institutions (hmm…..institution?), is the Goliath in a story of one family's long quest to find their own family member who died at Snake Hill and was buried there.

The "David" in this tale is a father and son descended of the dead man, Leonardo Andriani, who had died just days after being sent to the Lunatic Asylum due to what was most likely disorientation related to a stroke…….not mental illness.

While I have most often written about my (wild) Irish ancestral family, my father was born in Italy, coming to Jersey City with my dear Italian grandparents as a toddler in 1928. The story of Leonardo Andriani particularly resonates with me as both he and my Italian grandfather Giuseppe were veterans of the Italian military who fought in World War I. Leonardo was born in Italy in 1894 and Giuseppe was born there in 1898. As my grandmother Emanuela explained it to me, Italian WWI vets enjoyed "special" assistance should they want to emigrate to America.

Both Leonardo and my grandfather Giuseppe availed themselves of that "special" help and both came to New Jersey. Leonardo became a longshoreman in Hoboken. Giuseppe worked construction and did a good amount of "ditch-digging" in New York City according to family stories. Both men traveled home periodically to visit their wives and children in Italy, returning to America to earn more money in the hope of bringing their families to New Jersey.

My grandfather Giuseppe succeeded in doing that. Leonardo did not. His illness took him on a one-way trip to Snake Hill. His son did eventually make it to America and made a life here but the Andriani family did not know where Leonardo was laid to rest. Three decades later, Leonardo's grandson Patrick obtained his grandfather's death certificate and so started the quest to find Leonardo's grave at Snake Hill.

According to a piece written by Kristin Romey in 2005 for *The Archaeology Institute of America*:

"The turnpike authority was readying to petition Hudson County Supreme Court for permission to remove remains from the project area and reinter them in a mass grave in a nearby municipal cemetery when it discovered in the county archives the decades-old paper trail of Andriani's hunt for his grandfather. Since he was a direct lineal descendant of a possible individual the NJTA was preparing to disinter, the authority was legally obligated to inform

Andriani of their plans, and to name him as a plaintiff in the court petition. '[The NJTA] basically wanted to go in and rebury people without identifying them,' Andriani recalled. 'But if they found the cemetery, I wanted to find my grandfather.'

Andriani and the Turnpike authorities arrived at a court-approved agreement in January 2003: the NJTA would pay for a careful archaeological excavation that would enable identification of individual burials. The authority would also pay for the reinterment of all individuals and their personal effects, as well as a monument commemorating their reburial. It was an agreement that was to put into motion one of the largest, most complex disinterment projects in U.S. history."

Amazingly and against all odds due to the nature of the Snake Hill burial records, Leonardo Andriani's remains were found and identified. Most of the unearthed remains were not identified and while about 4,500 of the dead were disinterred and reburied at Maple Grove Park Cemetery in Hackensack, thousands more (the earliest of the burials at Snake Hill) remain abandoned in the old Snake Hill burial grounds.

Weehawken's Eldorado Park

One Sunday afternoon as I stood leaning against a wall near the information desk in the bustling NJ Transit concourse at New York Penn Station waiting for a train home, an anxious traveler asked the attendant: "Will all these people fit on the train?" That query caused me to involuntarily look up and, scanning the room, I noticed all the people decked out in Jets and Patriots football jerseys carrying everything from blankets to soft-side coolers filled with beer, headed for the stadium to join 70,000 fellow fans.

Open air venues offering excitement and all things entertaining are nothing new. Remember that old coliseum in Rome known for gladiator combat and wild animal hunts? Fun times for the spectators . . . not so much for the participants. In the 1890s, Hudson County had its own resplendent entertainment complex, Weehawken's Eldorado Park, boasting amphitheater, hotel, casino hosting indoor entertainment and dancing, restaurant, bandstand, castle, and 30 acres of magnificent grounds. The amphitheater seated 7,000, had a canvas roof that could be put up on rainy days and its enormous stage, over 300 feet long and 150 feet deep, accommodated a thousand performers at once. Perched atop the Palisades, with the entrance on Boulevard East in Weehawken, Eldorado Park offered visitors a panoramic view of the Hudson.

It was not uncommon for over 15,000 to visit the Park on any given day. To get them there, an elevated railway was built at the ferry station located below at the Hudson River's edge. Access to the elevated railway was via huge passenger elevators constructed to transport visitors up from the ferry house. Cost of all this? A half-million dollars or more.

So, what was drawing those 15,000 visitors and filling the amphitheater's thousands of seats? To describe the shows and performances as jaw-dropping spectacles is no overstatement or hyperbole. Bolossy Kiralfy, a famous international impresario of the day, produced the first glittering, epic amphitheater show, "King Solomon, or the Destruction of Jerusalem" complete with horse-drawn chariots, hundreds of ballet dancers, a trapeze artist diving off a tower 80 feet high into a net below, the Ali Baba troupe of acrobats and an evening that concluded with a spectacular fireworks display. Kiralfy's extravaganza was not without real-life drama on occasion.

One evening when Mr. James Mahoney, in his role as a charioteer, was driving a team of horses, a hissing calcium light spooked them and they bolted, pulling the chariot into a group of ballet dancers, knocking them down and leaving one girl with several broken ribs.

Bolossy Kiralfy

In August, 1893, the *New York Herald* reported a mishap under the headline "A Balloon's Mad Pranks." Eldorado Park often had hot air balloon entertainment with performers parachuting out after the balloon ascended heavenward. On that August evening, "aeronaut" Professor Le Strange ascended in his balloon, made his "daring leap from the clouds" and landed gracefully in the Hudson as winds had carried him over water. He was picked up by men in rowboats who anticipated where he would touch down. His balloon floated on in the prevailing breezes, heading straight for Manhattan's Tenderloin district. As it crossed over Manhattan, thousands on the sidewalks spotted it "belching forth a great volume of smoke." It passed over Broadway near 31st Street and was soon pursued by police from the 35th Street Station and over a 1,000 men and boys intent on bringing it down. The interstate journey ended when the balloon careened into the skylight of a hospital, smashing the glass but without any injuries to anyone inside. The police rolled up the wayward balloon, measuring about 45 feet high and 100 feet in circumference, and took it by wagon to their station house where a representative of the Eldorado Company came to reclaim it.

Despite its grandeur, spectacle and diversity of entertainment, attendance over time did not adequately cover the costs of operating the Eldorado. Ownership changed hands more than once and, in November, 1898, the casino was consumed by a catastrophic fire, brilliant flames lighting up the sky over the Hudson, not unlike the fireworks displays there years before.

Today, Eldorado Park is Eldorado Place, a tree-lined street of beautiful houses and home to Weehawken High School. While nothing is left from its days as an amusement park, a plaque erected by the Town Fathers on Boulevard East honors its memory and place in local history.

Votes for Women:

New Jersey Suffragettes

With the current state of national politics, the raging rhetoric and political pontification threatens to leave potential voters tone-deaf, disgusted, and dubious that their vote matters. That being said, it will do us all good to remember the struggle of one group of Americans desperate to have that right to vote: the ladies of the women's suffrage movement of the 19th and early 20th centuries.

As early as the 1850s, with the cry "Votes for Women," suffragettes banded together in pursuit of a place at the ballot box, led by movement pioneers Elizabeth Cady Stanton and Susan B. Anthony. Success remained elusive and as the quest for universal suffrage struggled on at the dawn of the 20th century, New Jersey's own Alice Paul became a committed and tireless leader in a new generation of women's rights advocates. While every successful cause has such indispensable and dedicated leaders, its followers are the wind beneath its wings, bringing energy and the power of numbers to the quest. We don't have to look any farther than our own New Jersey backyard to see that energy at work in the women's suffrage movement.

Alice Paul

In the second decade of the 1900s, one Hudson newspaper carried a column titled "Woman's Suffrage Forum," a regular feature that included information on local women's suffrage lectures, events, news and campaigns and also reported national progress as individual states voted for (or against) extending the right to vote to female residents. In 1915, New Jersey suffrage supporters succeeded in getting the question on a statewide referendum to be voted on in October of that year.

In August, as the election drew near and a woman's right to vote in New Jersey lay in the hands of the men of our state, the pages of local papers carried news of the upcoming arrival of the "suffrage torch" in Jersey City. The torch, symbolically unlit to represent the enlightenment that would come from granting we Jersey girls the right to vote, was to travel throughout the state to raise awareness and popular support for the upcoming suffrage amendment vote. The torch's travels across the Garden State were to be accompanied by celebrations and ceremonies attended by politicians, prominent citizens and the leaders and members of the Women's Political Union (WPU).

On August 7, 1915, the suffrage torch, accompanied by members of the New York contingent of the WPU, departed New York on the tugboat Holbrook and headed across the Hudson River. At the same time, representatives of the New Jersey WPU left Jersey City on the tug A.W. Smith, set to meet their New York sisters in the middle of the Hudson precisely at noon.

The torch handoff on the Hudson completed, the New Jersey delegation tug returned to the Pennsylvania Railroad pier after which a series of ceremonies and outdoor meetings were scheduled, the first starting at 1pm at Montgomery and Washington Streets.

The handoff and return of the banner-emblazoned tug with a member of the New Jersey delegation triumphantly holding up the suffrage torch were memorialized in two photographs that speak to the happy occasion and hopes for the upcoming special election.

Sadly, despite all their efforts, October did not bring the suffragettes a victory and the right to vote. Over 300,000 New Jersey men voted in the special election and while 42% of them were in favor of giving women the right to vote, the majority voted no and the amendment was defeated. Worse, that defeat meant the amendment could not be brought up for another vote in New Jersey for several years, a stinging blow to supporters of the suffrage movement.

Four years later, in October 1919, Mayor Frank Hague of Jersey City, representing New Jersey gubernatorial candidate Edward I. Edwards, addressed the executive committee of the New Jersey State Suffrage Association, a gathering that drew women from virtually every county in New Jersey.

Hague advised the women to emulate the recruiting methods of men's organizations and labor unions and to partner with the Democrats who had a "Votes for Women" plank in their platform, telling those present that the opportunity they had sought for years had finally come. In the end, the women of New Jersey won the right to vote when the 19th Amendment to the U.S. Constitution was approved by three-quarters of the states as of August 1920, one of those states being New Jersey.

Mayor Frank Hague

Post-Script: Ten days after the suffrage torch arrived in Hudson County and began its pilgrimage across New Jersey, it was stolen from the backseat of an automobile in Atlantic Highlands. The New Jersey WPU offered a reward of $50 for its safe return. Representatives of a New Jersey anti-suffrage group offered an additional $30 reward, keen to prove that the "anti-suffs" were not involved in the theft. A week later, a Wall Street lawyer named Lynch contacted the WPU saying he found the torch on a Philadelphia streetcar. The recovered torch safely made its way back to Newark and Mr. Lynch graciously refused to accept any reward.

This book is an anthology of the author's work as previously published in the RiverView Observer and on the author's blog-site (www.past-forward.com).

Images in this book are from the author's collection or public domain sources.

Front Cover Image: Giovanni Bruno, also known as John Brown, resident of Jersey City, NJ.

Back Cover Image: Jacob Reich and pals from Hudson County, NJ.

Made in the USA
Charleston, SC
22 February 2014